A Moral Philosophy for Management recog-nizes that the businessman confronts a potential dilemma: he must seek efficiency and profitability and square these goals with the Judaeo-Christian tradition and American democracy. To do so, he must guard against self-righteousness and cynicism while main-taining his technical capacity to run the company. On this basis the author defines the area of social responsibility natural to business, and shows how justice may be maintained.

Benjamin M. Selekman was Kirstein Professor of Labor Relations at the Graduate School of Business Administration, Harvard University. He is the author of "Labor Relations and Human Relations," and with Sylvia Selekman, co-author of "Power and Morality in a Business Society" (McGraw-Hill Paperbacks, 56079, $1.75).

A Moral Philosophy for Management

Benjamin M. Selekman

McGraw-Hill Book Company, Inc.
New York Toronto London

A MORAL PHILOSOPHY FOR MANAGEMENT

 Library of Congress Catalog Card Number 59-8562

II

To

Sylvia

Foreword

Stanley F. Teele, Dean
Graduate School of Business Administration
Harvard University

I AM GLAD that Professor Selekman has written this book. In doing so he has made a significant contribution to the growing discussion of the relationship of our rapidly changing business system to the newly emerging society of which it is so important a part.

Throughout our society thoughtful men are more and more turning their attention both to the values which command our loyalties and to the lack of clarity in men's minds about such values.

It is an oversimplification to observe that the tendency has been to keep concern with the practical everyday functioning of business completely apart from concern with ultimate values. Although many men have not made this separation, and others have done so only halfheartedly, it is nevertheless true that most businessmen, and indeed most academic economists, have spoken, written, and behaved as if these two concepts were worlds apart. They are not; and one deeply involved in business management knows they are not and cannot be.

At the Harvard Business School there is a clear beginning in efforts to help men think through for themselves appropriate reconciliations of the two concepts, and to find values which will help them achieve to the extent of their capacity. For many such men Professor Selekman's book will prove a useful and powerful stimulant. We need more books of this sort.

Preface

HAPPILY, the day is gone when business regarded labor as a commodity and the community as something outside its concern. As we advance into the twentieth century, spokesmen for industry are increasingly articulating a philosophy of moral and social responsibility.

At the same time, the fact must be faced that labor is a cost—indeed a major cost in doing business—and that the need to remain competitive and solvent places practical limits upon the social responsibilities a corporation may assume.

Thus the modern manager is continuously confronted by the necessity, on the one hand, of investing the power he wields with social and moral values if he is to hold it for any length and, on the other, of keeping his business productive and paying its way if he is to enjoy any opportunity at all to act responsibly.

This book is a modest attempt to explore this delicate balance—the basic social and moral requirements that must be met, the changes in attitude required, as well as the danger of overcommitment.

If I do not cite the vast ethical literature, both secular and religious, from ancient to modern times, it does not mean that I am not in its debt. I have been nurtured in the Judaeo-Christian tradition and I began the study of ethics in my youth, both in secular and religious schools. This essay does not, however, purport to be a study which applies ethical theories or religious doctrines to contemporary industrial life. Indeed, the thinking of this book has been shaped primarily by my experience as a student and teacher of labor relations during the past quarter-century at the Harvard Business School, and as an arbitrator, advisor, and administrator in industrial and communal affairs.

This experience sharpened a long-standing interest in the problem of power. Power is a strategic factor in labor relations, as it is in all human relations. Since power is both essential for human progress and at the same time potentially corrupting and destructive, I have in recent years devoted myself to an exploration of the relationship between power and morality. The first product of that concern was *Power and Morality in a Business Society*, published jointly with my late wife in 1956. It dealt with the broad phases of the problem as it applied to American society as a whole. This book, as the title suggests, concentrates upon management as a power group directing the economic life of the nation. Here is a new profession enjoying power on a scale hardly equalled in modern times. What account is it giving of itself as governors of men and institutions? What is the outlook for a socially responsible commitment?

Some of the ideas presented here were developed in a series of lectures and discussions as Walker-Ames Professor at the University of Washington in the spring of 1958. May I here acknowledge my gratitude for the opportunity to try out emerging thoughts in such a stimulating environment.

I wish also to thank the editors of the *Harvard Business Review* not only for permission to reprint articles which have appeared from time to time in that journal, but also for the fruitful collaboration I have enjoyed with them over the years.

Benjamin M. Selekman

Contents

PART IV · THE DANGER OF PERFECTIONISM

PART V · WANTED: A TECHNICAL FRAMEWORK

PART VI · WANTED: A MORAL FRAMEWORK

PART I

Moral Responsibility and Its Implications

1

Business in Search of a Moral Philosophy

WHAT will no doubt be recorded by historians as the ethical awakening of American business constitutes one of the dramatic developments of the past quarter-century. It has always been taken for granted that the American businessman was a moral and religious man, even though his daily practices might at times have been questioned. Up until recent years, however, it did not occur to businessmen to articulate the fact that what they did had moral goals. Now just the opposite is true. An explicit moral attitude is expressed again and again in literature, in meetings of business groups, in missions that go abroad, and in the reception of delegates who visit us to get a better understanding of American methods. The expression takes various forms. The social responsibility of business is a favorite theme; some leaders indeed take the unambiguous position that "the corporation is a moral community."

In one sense this articulation of a moral philosophy might be explained in terms of "industry in search of an ideology." Indeed, business has been under a grave handicap in that, unlike other groups in society, it has not been able to call itself a movement. Organized labor, for instance, is known as the labor movement—both as individual unions and as federations of unions. As a movement, labor conveys the implicit notion that it is devoted to the advancement of social goals. It is known as the main force behind social legislation and collective bargaining—both of which are committed to the improvement of conditions for the working people of the nation. It is significant that Labor Day is a national holiday, set aside to review the progress as well as the goals of labor in promoting social gains.

Not so with business. One never hears of a business movement or of an industrial movement, in the same sense that a union is part of a labor movement. Nor is any day set aside as a legal holiday to celebrate the achievements of industry. Every firm is an individual enterprise. Organized specifically for the purpose of turning out goods and services at a profit for particular stockholders, business can readily be seen as par excellence an individualistic institution. In fact, a company may be competitive not only with other firms in the same line but also with others making completely different products which can be substituted if price, quality, and delivery are attractive enough.

A change in the social and moral climate of our times has made it impossible to be content with letting matters rest at this point of competition and maximizing profits. Nowadays, individual institutions and national cultures are interrelated, and the ways in which American business has been characterized in the past are no longer adequate. Thus for a long time it was termed a form of private capitalism. But capitalism as we think of it is not a movement. It was Marxians, not American businessmen, who looked upon owners as an organized class with the purpose of exploiting labor at home and colonial empires abroad.

In recent years, businessmen have come to realize that they must find a way of interpreting themselves in a manner which would make our industrial system consistent with American democracy and the Judaeo-Christian tradition. Thus the term free enterprise system has come into use as a way of characterizing American business and industry. It is put forth as part of the American way of life. One of the basic tenets of those who advocate this system is that it allows for individualism; for individual businessmen to use their initiative to raise capital, to build plants, to engage labor, to market their product or service, all in competition with one another. But although superior to the old "tainted" term of capitalism, the free enterprise system still does not connote the idea of a movement in which people bind themselves together to transcend competitive interest in order to achieve a common goal.

So the search for a moral philosophy continues. Behind this search are two primary causes: the hostility directed against business beginning with the Great Depression of the thirties and the growth of a new professional management class, as distinguished from the owner-manager of former days, who built his own business, was the principal stockholder, and ran it either by himself or with those whom he took in as partners. Recent decades have witnessed a veritable explosion in business education, with large enrollments in business schools affiliated with universities. Association with a university immediately projects any calling on a technical and moral plane, with the challenge to meet standards already established in the older professions of law, medicine, engineering, architecture, the ministry, and teaching. With the concept of a profession comes also a self-consciousness, a desire to develop standards of technical performance as well as an ethical code, both of which give dignity and stature to those who enter the calling. Indeed, in every profession these two aspects have been implicit since the earliest days. Hence, the continuous debates on new vocations, whether they be teaching, social work, nursing, or business administration: are these professions or are they not?

Those steeped in the history of professions point out that no calling or vocation becomes a profession until it develops a body of knowledge, discipline, a method, and a code of professional ethics, transmittable and transmitted to successive generations largely through educational institutions and apprenticeship. And so, inevitably, schools of business and practitioners of management become concerned with ethical and moral codes.

The more imperative cause, however, behind the recent preoccupation with moral goals arises from the attack on business in the 1930s. Corporate executives found themselves called upon to defend their functions and to prove their usefulness to the community. Especially did this become urgent as the Roosevelt Administration enacted successive laws regulating major business activities, utilities, banks, exchanges, with a close scrutiny of the whole process of capitalization and sale of stock. Moreover, businessmen were singled out by the New Deal and Fair Deal under the articulate leadership of Presidents Roosevelt and Truman as being responsible for the debacle of the Depression. At the same time, legislation favorable to labor was enacted—social security, wages and hours, and the Wagner Act—which put the stamp of approval upon unions.

Thus, all of a sudden, business was dramatically at a disadvantage as compared to the position of power it had had before the 1930s. The Wagner Act, in particular, shook businessmen. Indeed, for two years, they and their lawyers held to the opinion that the Supreme Court would never validate the law. When, however, the Court upheld the Wagner Act, it became clear that industry had now to reconcile itself to the fact that it no longer possessed unilateral power, that henceforth it had to meet labor at least as an equal. Moreover, the tide of public opinion and the philosophy of those at the helm in Washington led government agencies to throw their weight behind the attempt of union leaders to organize the workers of the nation. Before long, an aggressive labor movement leaped into life and several million were enrolled in union ranks. This again proved a shock to corporate leadership. Unions now enjoyed an inside track with government. They asked for conditions of work spelled out in great detail in written contracts. Their demands were backed up by strikes, which again frequently enjoyed the support of the government.

Our entry into World War II accentuated the growth of trade unions. The government could not tolerate strikes either for higher wages or union security. There had to be some assurance that unions would be recognized by industry and that prices as well as wages would be regulated. The War Labor Board stabilized wage increases within defined limits and typically granted maintenance of membership and the checkoff of union dues when workers were organized and threatened to strike as negotiations broke down. Thus, when the war ended, some ten million American workers were organized into unions with strong leaders doing the bargaining for them.

Both in organizing campaigns and negotiations, these leaders attacked business as being primarily interested in profits rather than the welfare of the nation and its people. And so it became inevitable that if it was to maintain its position in the American community, corporate business had to develop a position of responsibility which would win it acceptance as a legitimate institution.

2

The Retreat from the Old Philosophy

It is difficult, if not almost impossible, for those who have come into adulthood during the past twenty-five years, to appreciate what a radical change this new attitude constitutes in the underlying posture and ideology of business. But to one who, like myself, grew up amidst coal and steel during the first two decades of the century, with short excursions among city sweatshops, the change is a dramatic one indeed. It can truly be said that in those early years business was indifferent if not callous to the welfare of the men and women employed in mines, mills, and factories.

The behavior of businessmen, however, was consistent with the basic philosophy dominating the nation. This philosophy was woven around four strands. Basic was the doctrine of Adam Smith, as formulated in *The Wealth of Nations*. Self-interest, he maintained, was the best guide to personal and social policy. In his reaction against the prevailing mercantilist or regulatory philosophy of government, Smith held that the wealth of a nation would be increased if government kept hands off and the energy and initiative inherent in individuals were mobilized in the pursuit of self-interest. If each man tried to gain as much as possible for himself by competing in the market place with others similarly motivated, the right price would be determined. It was the market place, with the bargaining of buyers and sellers as of workers and employers, that constituted a "self-regulator." Meanwhile, under the prod of self-interest, each individual would try to create and produce as much as possible. Thus, the wealth of the nation would be enhanced.

It is to be noted that under this philosophy, wages constitute a price, just like that of any inanimate goods. Thus labor was considered a commodity; the employer had no responsibility to pay more than the competition of the market determined.

The second strand in our economic and social philosophy was contributed by Malthus. Population tended to increase much more rapidly than the food supply—at a geometric as compared to an arithmetic ratio. The workingman was thus foredoomed to live close to a subsistence level. Wages, consequently, could not possibly rise much above the level required for mere maintenance.

Ricardo added a third strand—or perhaps formulated Smith's and Malthus's analysis in more "elegant" language. Following closely the workings of the market place, he formulated the iron law of wages: wages could never be more than that amount required to yield subsistence. This famous iron law of wages was later used by Karl Marx as proof of the exploitative character of capitalism; it was to become one of his most potent weapons in arousing hostility toward private industry and winning adherents for his revolutionary strategy calling for the violent overthrow of the existing order and the seizure by the proletariat of the means of production and distribution.

After the middle of the century, Darwin's discoveries about the struggle for survival in nature were used as the basis for what has come to be called Social Darwinism. Given its most systematic expression by Herbert Spencer, it meant that, as in nature, so with man: only the fittest survived. The strong rose to leadership; the poor were submerged. The iron law of wages and the other adverse conditions of the poor were just another aspect of the order of nature. It followed that employers and industrialists had to take very little responsibility for improving the living conditions of their workers.

Back of all this—and indeed preceding nineteenth-century economics and social philosophy—was the traditional philosophy of the Poor Law, particularly as amended in 1834. To give help to the poor was only to degrade them, to pauperize them. Public relief was demoralizing at best; to give outdoor relief to the poor, that is to say, aid in their own homes, was decried as an incentive toward shiftlessness and indolence. If people were so badly off they could not take care of themselves, they should be put in the poorhouse or some other type of institution. Such charity as was justified had better be administered by private relief agencies; for these would emphasize "character"; to the extent that the individuals were redeemable and could be rehabilitated, they would be helped. Otherwise they would be left to shift for themselves or admitted to almshouses.

As a matter of fact, this philosophy of deterrence prevailed in England pretty well into the first decade of the twentieth century, when the Liberal party under the leadership of Asquith, Lloyd George, and Churchill enacted unemployment insurance. They thus initiated the beginning of what was to become a comprehensive social insurance program. By the 1940s Beveridge's proposed "cradle-to-the-grave" assistance became the basic program of the British government regardless of the party in office.

In this country, the deterrent poor-law philosophy, interrelated with the economic teachings of Adam Smith, Malthus, and Ricardo, and with the biological doctrines of Darwin, prevailed until the 1930s, when it gave way under the impact of the Great Depression to the comprehensive program of Federal assistance and insurance already alluded to, as well as to regulatory legislation of business and to protective laws for labor and farmer. It marked the advent of the welfare state in full panoply, as contrasted with its gradual development in Britain, over more than a quarter of a century.

Nor was this change of philosophies readily accepted in this country. On the contrary, it met strong—at times bitter—resistance by industry and conservative elements. In fact, in the early stages of the New Deal, the Supreme Court took the traditional line of declaring such welfare legislation unconstitutional on the grounds that it was reserved to the states: the Federal government enjoyed only those functions actually defined. Relief measures and social security legislation were beyond these defined powers; they belonged to the reserved powers withheld by the several states when the Constitution was ratified.

Such indeed had been the traditional doctrine of the Supreme Court as well as previous administrations. Thus in 1852, President Pierce vetoed an act of Congress which would have set aside public land to be sold to make funds available for the establishment of mental hospitals, an act passed as a result of the persistent agitation of Dorothea Dix, who was outraged by the way in which the mentally sick were treated in almshouses and jails. Pierce based his veto on the doctrine of limited power under the Constitution; eleemosynary matters were reserved to local government. Similarly, Cleveland later vetoed an act of Congress making available free grain to farmers who had suffered during a drought, reasoning that such action was within the province of the several states.

After President Roosevelt threatened to appoint additional judges, Chief Justice Hughes led the Supreme Court in a series of epoch-making decisions that reversed traditional policy and declared constitutional, under the power to regulate interstate commerce, welfare as well as regulatory legislation enacted in the early years of the New Deal. From the point of view of constitutional history, these decisions upholding Federal supremacy in social and economic matters marked a complete reversal of policy.

The position of business, especially Big Business, sank to a nadir during the 1930s. Indeed, businessmen were being replaced in the esteem of the populace by a new middle class made up of workers, union leaders, and farmers. Wage earners, in particular, were emerging from their lowly status which they had occupied traditionally as immigrants.

During the first half of the nineteenth century these immigrants came from the West European nations; most of them were Anglo-Saxons, Irish, Germans, or Scandinavians. These men and women had little difficulty in winning acceptance before long as Americans. In contrast was the lot of those who came in the latter half of the nineteenth century and in the early twentieth, a veritable tidal wave from East Europe and the Mediterranean region, Slavs, Russians, Italians, Czechs, Hungarians, Greeks, and so on. They could not speak the language, and their customs were strange to the sons of the earlier immigrants who were now settled in the country and had become the employers or "bosses" of the new "aliens" in their daily work. But with the cessation of immigration in 1914, these new immigrants also gradually became adapted to the new country. This was especially true of their children as they went through our schools and colleges. The Depression of the 1930s, with its large-scale unemployment, stirred millions of people to become conscious of their American citizenship and their rights. It was they who were mobilized by Roosevelt and Truman in the support of the New and Fair Deal. Thus this erstwhile alien population which made up the hard core of the American proletariat achieved a new status. Their spokesmen, men like Hillman, Dubinsky, Lewis, Meany, Murray, Curran, and Reuther, supplanted the "tycoons" and men of traditional privilege as the new wielders of power on the industrial front, in the halls of Congress and legislatures, and in the executive suites of the While House and state capitals.

With the attack on Pearl Harbor and our entry into the war, the mood of the nation changed. All this led to an abatement of the attack on business. For one thing, President Roosevelt put the winning of the war first and internal reform second. Moreover, under government direction corporations converted themselves into arsenals, and before long, the very flow of war material overshadowed the inadequacies brought to the surface by the Depression. What is more, chronic unemployment, some ten million as late as 1940, soon gave way to labor shortages, tight labor markets, and full employment. Finally, the various war agencies, and in particular the War Labor Board, succeeded in integrating rapidly growing militant unions into the industrial framework of the country. To be sure, union recognition, maintenance of membership, and the checkoff were typically granted to unions. Nevertheless, what might have been serious industrial conflict was avoided. An accommodation, though an imposed one, was achieved.

At the conclusion of the war, industry-wide strikes occurred in steel, coal, meat packing, and railways, as well as in some major corporations like General Motors. It was a period of transition from war to peace. Corporations and unions were now left to their own negotiations, instead of following the lead of the War Labor Board. When they failed to agree on the amount of wage increase, however, President Truman intervened when strikes were declared and either by himself or through fact-finding boards virtually continued to impose a wage settlement, to be followed immediately by a price increase approved again by the White House. The first postwar year, 1945–1946, was indeed a turbulent year in industrial relations, marking the largest number of working days lost through strikes in our history. It also marked the beginning of the postwar inflationary trend.

3

The New Posture of Business and Its Implications

BY 1947 a reaction had set in. Labor and the New and Fair Deal were losing favor with the nation. With war and postwar prosperity and high earnings, the privations of the Depression began to dim in memory. The aggressive tactics of John L. Lewis and the nationwide strikes in steel and other essential industries turned public opinion to the right. Senator Taft became a vigorous spokesman for the conservative opposition. The enactment of the Taft-Hartley Act slowed down the growth of unions and, indeed, imposed restrictions upon the freedom that they had had under the Wagner Act. They too had now to avoid unfair labor practices.

The election of Eisenhower to the Presidency and the return of the Republican party to office was a defeat for labor. Whether or not it marked, at the same time, the ascendancy of business to its pre-1930 position is another question. But at least it did change the political climate from that of hostility to friendliness toward business. Indeed, prominent corporate executives like Wilson of General Motors, Humphrey of the Hanna interests, and Weeks, who was close to New England business enterprise, were appointed to the Cabinet.

Meanwhile the business community itself, through its organizations and spokesmen, increasingly articulated a philosophy of ethical and moral responsibility. In the cold war with Russian communism, as had been true in the actual war with Nazi Germany, private business saw itself as part and parcel of the democratic free world, in contrast to the government-dominated industries in Fascist and Communist nations.

Unanswered Questions

In its eagerness to associate itself with social and moral goals, business has failed to recognize that it has been turning its back on the rationale underlying its existence during the nineteenth century, the market place which Adam Smith envisioned as the automatic regulator of wages, prices, and conditions of work and life. Indeed, thus far business and its spokesmen have evolved no substitute for the economic philosophy of Adam Smith, under which they were freed from personal responsibility. The pursuit of self-interest under competitive conditions was precisely the very thing they were supposed to do if they would best serve the nation.

Nor has business thought through the implications that go with the assumption of moral and social responsibility. For business is a power system; it brings together and coordinates capital, science, people, machinery, resources, and markets in order to produce and distribute goods and services. As a power organization it is just like science—neither moral nor immoral; it is amoral. For power is energy mobilized to achieve certain ends. This energy in itself is neutral as far as ethical values are concerned. It is only as power becomes involved with human beings, that moral considerations develop. Since, however, one's own conscience frequently becomes clouded in the application of moral criteria, other power systems develop, which challenge and check the business administrator just as he challenges and checks the wielders of authority in rival power systems, such as trade unions, government agencies, farm associations, and so on. In meeting and negotiating with the other power groups as well as in making internal decisions, business is always confronted with the task of keeping its power—that is to say, its authority—at a high level of productivity.

The one test of its productivity is competitiveness and profitability. No matter how high its moral intentions, a corporation may not survive long unless it can produce goods and services which the community will buy in a competitive market, at a price which will pay bills, provide for depreciation, and at the same time yield a profit. Thus almost every important act of a corporation executive creates a situation of tension—what I like to refer to as "the technical *must* versus the ethical *ought*."

The assumption of moral and social responsibility raises searching questions for the men in charge of business. It calls for a quality of character and, at times, an internal conversion not easy to achieve. The executive and his associates must be willing to assume and exercise authority. As such they must be competitive, full of drive, on the alert for new ideas, and firm with those who do not pull their oar in the enterprise. At the same time, they must exercise authority without becoming punitive, capricious, unjust, self-righteous, cynical, or, at the worst, corrupt—pitfalls which always lie hidden to trap those who wield power.

Beyond these matters of personal involvement, how great a moral commitment should business be expected to make? Surely we do not expect a business to be conducted like a Sunday School or a family. Does management now have available the tools that it needs to organize and govern an efficient, as well as a socially satisfying, human institution? If the tools are now inadequate, along what direction must they be made more effective?

One warning must always be kept in mind. The search for moral goals cannot lightly be used as a form of public relations. Once businessmen invoke ethical and social values they are tampering with the most sacred symbols of human society. One can exploit a product or service, emphasize its style, utility, price, beauty, the prestige it may bring, and so forth. In the market place, materialism has its natural habitat. The consumer may buy or refuse to buy. But morality is the most treasured possession of a people, hammered out over history as man searches for some satisfying answer to the puzzlement inhering in his relationship to his fellow man and to his God. These values are the ones for which men die, for which martyrs have given their lives.

All of which underscores the grave responsibility which businessmen are undertaking in espousing moral and ethical goals in the actual conduct of business. It is in a sense a fearful undertaking. If failure ensues, then faith in our type of civilization may well suffer irreparable damage.

What we shall, therefore, attempt to explore in this book is how much of a moral obligation business can and should assume and how best to fulfill such an obligation.

First, let us examine the pitfalls in behavior that management must avoid in the daily conduct of industry.

4

Community and Communion or Alienation and Divisiveness?

BUSINESSMEN have been talking about a concern for human relations and a concept of social and moral responsibility for the last several years, but at times their statements and actions based on economic and political views have sharply contradicted the moral philosophy they profess in speeches and articles. This conflict, if indefinitely continued, may well alienate their employees and frustrate their attempt to surround business activity with moral sanctions. Although they may handle any individual employee as a human being, they think of labor in general as an abstraction.

For instance, businessmen give labor little or no credit for increasing the nation's productivity. They put the whole blame for inflation on unions. They regard labor as a cost to be reduced as far and as rapidly as possible. They are confused and contradictory with regard to government, often seeking favors for themselves but protesting efforts to help others. And they dismiss union leaders as "just politicians," overlooking their own role as politicians.

If this tendency continues, we may end up with a class alignment in American industry—something that all the agitation of the most zealous Communists has so far failed even to get off the ground, let alone accomplish. Would it not be one of the tragic ironies of history if management itself, while striving to bring about that social unity implicit in true morality, actually perpetrated that divisiveness which Karl Marx, more than 100 years ago, predicted would soon excite the proletariat to overthrow their "capitalist masters"?

Threat of Divisiveness

Not that businessmen are guilty of insincerity in trying to give their lives some moral significance. They have done much for individual employees by encouraging counseling and other new social and psychological approaches which are generally called "human relations."

As for the wide concern with the crisis confronting contemporary man, business leaders have placed themselves in the very vanguard of those seeking social and moral answers. In contrast with the nineteenth and early twentieth centuries, when *caveat emptor,* rugged individualism, and "public be damned" were the prevailing attitudes, recent years have witnessed a more and more willing acceptance by the modern corporation of a social responsibility to its employees and, indeed, to the whole community.

Consistent with this moral quest, industrial leaders have put their weight behind the world-wide struggle for liberty and justice. Wherever businessmen gather, this theme of social responsibility is sure to receive major attention.

So it is ironical, or maybe pathetic, that businessmen may at the same time be acting unthinkingly to create a class society, with all the threats to democracy and moral life which that implies.

It is hard to believe, even for a moment, that the extreme danger of irreconcilable class struggle in the Marxian sense can ever overtake us in America. But we must not be too sure of our immunity. Society is a fragile thing in many ways, and history has a way of taking unexpected turns and twists. Who could have known fifty years ago that communism would come first to Russia, an agricultural, precapitalist country, instead of to England or Germany, both highly industrialized, fully developed capitalist nations? Who would have foreseen that China, even more primitive industrially than Russia, would be the next large nation to go communist? Who would have predicted that the United States would break her strongly rooted tradition of isolationism to take the lead in a world-wide coalition against the further spread of communism?

But even if we escape an out-and-out class struggle, the danger of divisiveness still remains.

Avoiding a class society is one of the most difficult endeavors in human history. In fact, few nations have succeeded in escaping this dilemma—from ancient Israel, Greece, and Rome down to the modern western nations, including Russia. Israel may have had no native slave class, but must have practiced slavery; by Biblical injunction, native Hebrews had to be freed "on the seventh year." Ancient Athens never freed even high-talented Greek slaves who contributed to her culture. European nations still have their nobility, middle, and lower classes. Russia has its élite of the Politburo, party functionaries, commissars, and so forth.

We in America, while experiencing normal "social climbing," have been fortunate so far in preventing our society from being structured into class and caste. The Supreme Court has recently given the *coup de grâce* to the one exception, the Negro; although the going is rough at the moment, no American doubts the final outcome.

Also in organizational work, we rely on hierarchies to provide authority and discipline. Or, to put it another way, the fact that people recognize the legitimacy of superior positions makes it possible to get the world's work done with a minimum of resistance. In churches we have archbishops, bishops, ministers, and deacons; in colleges we have presidents, vice-presidents, deans, professors, and instructors; in business we have chairmen, presidents, vice-presidents, department managers, and foremen.

This sort of social structure, therefore, is natural and organic; it need give us little concern. What should concern us is the kind of class society which Karl Marx and Friedrich Engels envisioned in *The Communist Manifesto*—a supposedly inevitable class struggle leading eventually to the revolt of the masses—or a division in industry creating an elite which looks down on those who do the daily work.

Moral Objectives

Such an attitude denies the moral objectives which business is striving to attain. What are these objectives, what are these ethical goals? Gross exploitation of women and child labor, long hours of work under harsh, unsafe conditions, and lack of any provision against unemployment or old age—those were the social problems of a generation ago. Today we are confronted with moral dilemmas arising from complex problems of power. Managerial authority is challenged by strong unions and by a critical, if not hostile, government. It is much easier to dispense justice, to be benevolent, than it is to share power—especially with those who have the means to compel such sharing.*

Yet such sharing lies at the core of our Judaeo-Christian tradition and of the American democratic credo. Basic to this ethic is the dignity of man, the equality of all men in the eyes of God, and the common brotherhood of all men as children of God. We also think in terms of equality of opportunity: everyone is not born equal in ability, but everyone should have an equal chance to fulfill himself.

Finally, we hold strongly to a sense of community, of fellow-

* See Sylvia Selekman and Benjamin Selekman, *Power and Morality in a Business Society*, McGraw-Hill Book Company, Inc., New York, 1956.

ship, indeed of communion. We aspire to a moral climate in which community and communion are interchangeable, in which we all share the glory as well as pain, the gains as well as the sacrifices of a democratic, Judaeo-Christian nation. These concepts and feelings derive from the great sacred documents—the Ten Commandments, the Sermon on the Mount, the teachings of saints and rabbis. They find their secular echo in the Declaration of Independence, Lincoln's Gettysburg Address, the Preamble to the Constitution, and other state papers that have become hallowed in time.

In common with other Americans, businessmen subscribe unequivocally to these tenets. Yet when talking about actual problems such as productivity, inflation, and the related political activities of union and government, they unwittingly undercut their own professions of faith.

5

Credit for Productivity

IF THERE is one achievement for which the United States is receiving world-wide applause, it is industrial productivity. However critical of us our enemies and at times even our friends may be, they are unanimous in their admiration for the way we have succeeded in turning out goods and services in such ever-increasing volume at prices which enable the common man to enjoy the good things of life.

Their admiration—and appreciation—began during the war, when our "arsenal of democracy" saved our allies from what looked like defeat after Dunkirk, the fall of France, and Hitler's invasion of Russia. From that day to this, delegation after delegation has visited us from all over the world to learn our secret. Productivity centers are springing up in Europe and Asia, with our help and guidance. We bring hope that the age-old struggle to rescue the masses of the world from poverty can be won and that standards of living and well-being throughout the world can be raised. For the first time in our history, we are bringing forth living proof that the poor need *not* always be with us.

Leaving Labor Out

Our achievement is great by any standard, historical or contemporaneous. Yet it is right here that American management may be committing a major blunder. For the tendency is to deny labor any important role in, or credit for, this achievement. When unions come in during negotiations and argue for a wage increase saying, "We've increased productivity so-and-so much," the reply may well be, "Why, we went out and got the capital; we built the plants; we bought the tools; we launched merchandising and sales campaigns; we created the markets. You do less now than before. Machines do the work; all you have to do is to tend them." Management forgets that the "all you do" is all-important.

To illustrate, recently I visited a progressive company. The management group, from the president to the foremen, were alert, full of drive, anxious to be good citizens in all relationships. This was a growth industry, in which automation had made rapid strides. It could be truly said that machines were doing most, if not quite all, of the work. A wage negotiation was pending, and management personnel were sounding off to me on the fallacies underlying the union arguments for an increase, one of which was credit for increased productivity.

A long weekend was looming up, and I thought I might find it profitable to spend the time in one of the plants, instead of the city where corporation headquarters were located, since this was a continuous operation with automated or semiautomated machines going around the clock. I was surprised to find the general manager, the superintendent, and two assistant superintendents all on hand. Something had gone wrong. The machines were not processing the raw materials. The executives had to forego their weekend plans.

The executives were busy telephoning their mechanics, many of whom were either not at home or did not care to give up their holiday even at overtime rates. The men had to be called according to the rules of the contract—those lowest on the overtime roster had to be called first—and that took time. To make it more difficult, many of the men had jobs on the side, since they worked a five-day week, and the eight-hour day ended at 3:30 or 4 P.M.

Nevertheless, with persistence, a crew of mechanics was mobilized, and before long they had the plant going again. The supervisors and the men returned home to enjoy their weekend, with the dials oscillating beautifully around the proper pressures. Automation was king once more.

Each Doing His Part

What is the lesson of all this? For one thing, in a modern complex organization it is almost impossible to pin down who *really* is responsible for productivity. In a literal sense, major credit should go to scientists: the physicists, chemists, mathematicians, and engineers. They are the ones who make the basic discoveries about the power of nature, how to harness it and turn it into energy to be used by man for his ends. The rest of us exploit their findings.

Without management, however, scientific findings might never get out of the laboratory. For management obtains the capital, builds factories, buys raw materials and machines, hires labor, advertises and sells, and so on. It organizes the production and distribution of finished products; it also encourages research. Nevertheless, no one in management, from the president on down, is responsible in a fundamental sense for the dynamic factors in increasing productivity as much as the scientists, engineers, and technicians.

The fact of the matter is that productivity is the result of a complex cooperative effort under the leadership of management. The difficulty of identifying the specific individuals who play the key role in productivity was brought home vividly to me during the war. I was visiting Detroit and was much impressed by the way Pratt and Whitney engines for bombers were being turned out in automobile plants. These engines, once meticulously hand tooled, were being mass-produced in large numbers by new employees possessing no special skills, sometimes with no previous experience working in a factory.

"If you had to single out any individuals responsible for this conversion, who would they be?" I inquired. The answer came back, "The master mechanics." Here were the men who possessed the skill necessary to diagnose the handmade engine, break it down into parts, make the drawings for special tools, lay out the work, the sequence of the various processes, and the assemblies, until the completed engines came off in rapid succession as finished products, ready for inspection, shipping, and mounting. To me, master mechanics have ever been the unsung heroes of war and peace!

The real point, of course, is that not even the master mechanics deserved all the credit for these engines. The drive to greater productivity, to tinkering with machinery, to beating a competitor or rival with a better method, has seized Americans from the beginning. It is a national trait, our way of expressing a "will to power." In any given operation, everyone plays his part in achieving the final goal. No group—including management—has the right to arrogate to itself major credit or to deny to any other group its part, however humble, in achieving what is essentially a cooperative result.

Management must be particularly careful not to stamp a differential status on various groups working in industry. Against such a background, all the speeches and communications about the free enterprise system sound like the tinkling of hollow brass, and management cannot then contribute to the welding of a community, to the inspiring of communion.

6

Blaming Labor for Inflation

WHEN we come to the problem of inflation, the prevailing attitude of businessmen, with a few notable exceptions, is just the same but in the contrary direction: labor is to blame. By now the charge is oft-repeated and familiar: strong unions directed by power-driven labor leaders, competing with one another, make exorbitant demand after exorbitant demand at each negotiation, not only for substantial wage increases but also for a variety of fringe benefits—which together exceed the annual increase in productivity. Since the unions can shut down a whole industry or single out one corporation for a threatened shutdown, management has no alternative but to yield.

The increased cost cannot be met by increased productivity; hence it must be passed on through increases in price. Thus, inflation gets a push upward. This whole tendency is aggravated by the escalator principle guaranteeing wage increases as the consumers' price index goes up—a formula embodied in many labor agreements these days—really a type of built-in inflation.

An example of this argument appears in the annual report of the United States Steel Corporation for 1956: *

* "Financial Summary: As Wage Inflation Goes . . . ," *Annual Report of the United States Steel Corporation*, 1956, p. 25.

This current evidence supplements other reasons for believing that cost-price inflation is in danger of becoming a permanent feature of American life. Central to such a conclusion is the fact that the vast power of industry-wide labor unions in compelling annual increases in employment costs far beyond increases in productivity is automatically compelling inflation. This is because, up and down the industrial production line, employment cost constitutes, directly or indirectly, the vast bulk of all costs.

There is thus a natural sequence between the basic employment cost inflation and the cost-covering price inflation since the latter is but the reflection of the former. To the extent that product price increases are eventually reflected in cost-of-living indexes, further employment cost increases are automatically generated by reason of so-called cost-of-living clauses in wage contracts. This starts the process all over again.

Inevitability of Pressure

But what are these unions? They are not abstractions; they are made up of individual workers, with families and community attachments, responding normally to sales promotion to enjoy all the good things which American industry turns out so abundantly. No individual, be he a worker at the bench, a college professor, or a company president, ever thinks of his own wage or salary in terms of its impact on inflation or deflation.

Take the case of teachers, who have suffered more than anyone else from the shrinking value of the dollar. If college professors knew a way of remedying the situation short of shutting down classrooms by strikes, they certainly would give no thought to the possible aggravation of inflation consequent upon increases in their salaries.

As for management personnel, the record attests to its sustained preoccupation with executive compensation over the last twenty-five years, a preoccupation growing out of the desire to reward executive talent adequately. In view of the steep taxes which take such a large "bite" out of salaries, a comprehensive and rather generous program has been worked out in most corporations providing not only substantial annual salaries but also stock options, pensions, lifetime contracts with deferred annuities, payments to widows in case of early, unexpected death, consultantship after retirement, and so forth. Let the companies and individuals concerned ask themselves whether, and to what extent, the query is ever raised as to how these plans affect the inflationary spiral!

Nor let it be thought for a moment that hourly paid production workers are unaware of what is going on at the top levels. Let me illustrate with a personal experience. I recently interviewed personnel at various levels in a relatively isolated community. Shortly before my visit, the president of the company, wanting to keep in touch with his people, had stopped off on his way to a national meeting. He met with union members, among others. This was not a "power-driven" CIO or AFL union but an independent union, an outgrowth of a company union. A negotiation for a wage increase was pending, and, as usual these days, management was critical of the union demand as inflationary.

This executive had been articulate in warning against the inflationary danger of repeated rounds of wage increases. His own salary was in six figures. He also enjoyed stock options, a long contract, pensions, and consultantship after retirement. Incidentally, his contract also carried an escalator clause.

Since compensation of this dimension is open to public scrutiny, the men knew all these details. They thought that their president had done pretty well for himself. Indeed, they considered him so skillful a negotiator that, so I was told, they had invited him to become their representative if he ever felt like resigning his company office!

This man is not being overpaid in his market. But when neither he nor his associates are ever troubled by the impact of his relatively generous compensation on inflation, how can anyone expect the carpenter, the painter, the bricklayer, the tailor, the coal miner, or the steel worker to worry about the impact of a 6 per cent to 10 per cent hourly increase in any one year or sometimes every other year? He too is enjoying a favorable market, just like the executive, indeed the best he has ever enjoyed.

It would be salutary if business executives conceived of unions as marketing agencies made up of men and women engaged in a common craft or industry who look to their salesmen (the Reuthers and the MacDonalds) to get for them the maximum price obtainable in the market for their only commodity, skill. To be sure, union leaders are ambitious and rivalrous and indulge in plenty of politics. These ambitions and rivalries, however, must be expressed in terms of the expectancies of the people they represent. Otherwise, opposition develops and the ranks break away.

Chasing Living Costs

On my field trips, I spent considerable time talking with employees as well as with supervisors. "What are your problems here?" is a query I put to them. "Our company's not bad," is a typical reply. "We have our problems. We have our differences. Once in a while things get a bit tough. But on the whole we iron things out. Our real quarrel is not with the company but with the economy. There is something wrong. We're always chasing the increased cost of living. No sooner do we get a wage increase than up go prices. We're always behind. We're always chasing a bigger grocer and butcher bill."

I have tried to explain the economics of inflation to these people. I find them incredulous when I point out that economists and others believe that they and their unions play a primary role in pushing prices upward. What they ask for seems so justified and modest to them; if anyone is to blame in their eyes, it is management, for adding not only the actual wage increase to cost but a generous amount on top.

Right or wrong, I am convinced that there is no way of stopping employees from expecting—indeed from demanding—a wage increase when the cost of living is going up, and as long as they respond in typical American fashion to advertising and merchandising. They believe in and want a rising standard of living.

After all, we practice and encourage obsolescence on a huge scale. We continuously enlarge our markets and thus supply one of the dynamics for our material growth. But by the same token, we also may be putting upward pressure on the price level.

Thus, we provide consumer credit to enable people to buy on deferred payments new and better goods and services, and such credit may give impetus to the inflationary spiral. And as we increase our markets, we expand capacity and so build new plants, buy new equipment, enlarge our sales organizations, and so forth. Some of the materials we want are scarce, as is labor. So we bid up prices and wages—the latter not infrequently above the union rate, to the embarrassment of the union official. Labor piracy is not an unknown practice when the prospects for profits are good. In my own experience, unions have frequently acted as a restraining or at least a moderating influence. I am convinced that in boom times wages, especially for skilled craftsmen, would rise much faster without unions than they now do. One has only to reflect on what has happened during the past twenty-five years to the wages of domestic help, a completely unorganized group.

It is about time for all hands to agree that few individuals are so self-denying as voluntarily to forego a wage or salary increase at a time when, on the basis of demand for their services in a free society, it is entirely justified. It would take a superhuman effort to think of such remuneration in terms of its potential effect on prices. Granted that a million automobile workers grouped together in a union obtaining simultaneous wage increases are bound to exert a greater impact on pricing policy than similar increases obtained by executives, that the total amount of money is much greater, as is the percentage of total cost, and that pressure can be exercised by the union through threat of a strike. The fact remains that basic *motivation* is the same for worker as for executive. They are both simply taking advantage of a favorable market.

This motivation has nothing to do with the fact that wages have been going up faster than productivity. The fact that man-hour productivity increases annually by 2 to 3 per cent on the average is simply a statistical datum, significant for discussion, research, and high-level policy, but irrelevant to anyone's personal course of life.

Equality of Sacrifice

Let me say one thing further. If we expect people ever to forego wage increases, it will have to be the result of a moral crusade, started not by those at the bottom but by those at the very top of the economic and social scale. The example would have to be set by presidents, vice-presidents, and all other executives. It would have to be so dramatic a crusade as to move people to make a great material sacrifice in order to save the solvency of the nation. Nor should we use the word *sacrifice* lightly. It surely would be a sacrifice for the president of a company to forego an increase voted by the board of directors as a reward for his stewardship. Nevertheless, without this sacrifice it would be useless to expect the sweeper, the carpenter, or the electrician to forego the relatively modest wage increase he might win in a given year.

To be sure, in a number of negotiations in recent years management has attempted to bring to the fore the relationships between wages, prices, costs, and therefore, inflation. For instance, in 1952, Benjamin Fairless promised that the United States Steel Corporation would forego a price increase if the unions would forego a wage increase. But this proposal did not touch the heart of the matter. It called for a sacrifice on the part of the workers as individuals, with no similar sacrifice on the part of managers as individuals. Whether prices went up or not would not be a controlling factor in determining executive salaries. That would depend on profitability. The only tenable moral position would have been to declare that everybody was involved in the dangers of inflation and so must take a similar vow and similar action to prevent a common danger from becoming a national disaster.

The problem is aggravated by the fact that present-day management is no longer an owning group. Executives are hired as is labor. They do not enjoy the moral sanctions that went with ownership. They have made fewer sacrifices, if any, for the business, and therefore their claims on it are more limited.

It may well be that we have never made the transition in moral framework to accompany the change in ownership and managership of American industry. Typically, the president of a company still acts as if he were the chief owner. He surrounds his office with the same symbols and rewards which adhered to his predecessor-owner. In particular, he applies to himself the yardstick of chief owner with regard to compensation, bonuses, stock ownership, and safeguards for himself and his family after retirement. At the same time, he exploits the new framework of professional management when defending himself against attack by labor or government, by pointing out that management serves really as a professional administrator, that it represents not only stockholders, or owners, but also customers, suppliers, and employees, that as such it tries to balance the legitimate interests of all these groups.

Since in the final analysis private enterprise must find moral justification to be acceptable to the community, it is exceedingly important that business executives take great care to avoid the appearance of sponsoring double standards and an atmosphere of divisiveness. Inflation is indeed a menacing danger. But we will get nowhere by blaming workers or their unions any more than businessmen or their corporations. Nor will preaching self-restraint to individuals and their leaders get us very far.

It boils down to this: either we all make a voluntary sacrifice together—and I doubt this is a practical measure—or government must introduce those fiscal and monetary measures which will really make sacrifice as equal and uniform as possible. We may in this way slow down the boom prosperity we have been enjoying these past years with all its euphoria, but we will be more certain of our savings, our insurance policies, and our pensions. Of course, we also run the risk, as Sumner Slichter * has warned us rather persuasively, in my opinion, of creating unemployment as well as of restoring the violent cyclical swings of the past with no assurance of avoiding inflation over the long pull.

"No Work, No Pay"

In addition to the divisive attitudes pivoting around national economic issues there are several other long-standing positions not altogether consistent with a morality which calls for human dignity and fellowship in a common community.

One of these, that wages are a variable cost, is undergoing modification under our very eyes. Compared to plant and machinery, which are considered as fixed costs and maintained and replaced as needed, labor has been traditionally engaged by the hour, or by the task, and paid only when working. We have been witnessing in our generation a dramatic shift in the direction of making the human cost of labor more and more a charge of industry. This is a natural objective of trade unions as marketing agencies for workers and is an attractive vote getter for political parties and politicians.

Accordingly, union contracts have been extended to embrace such provisions as call-in pay, separation allowances, supple-

* "Thinking Ahead: On the Side of Inflation," *Harvard Business Review,* September–October, 1957, p. 15.

mentary unemployment benefits, sick and hospitalization benefits, paid vacations, and pensions. The same drive lies behind all the government measures that go under the term social security. So strong is the momentum of this shift of sentiment that the Eisenhower Administration, though critical of what the Roosevelt and Truman regimes had done, actually has enlarged the scope of expenditures on this score. If human life is to be regarded as precious, and every individual is to be entitled to equal treatment as a member of the American community, what other alternative has industry but to make human labor a fixed cost?

Mobility and Community

The traditional economic doctrine that labor is or should be a highly mobile factor in production is also being modified. The workingman is supposed to be ready and willing to move about from location to location as need for his labor shifts. Thus a major argument advanced against company-financed security programs, such as pensions and supplementary unemployment benefits, is the "danger" that they may freeze men on their jobs and make them reluctant to migrate to those areas where they may be in demand.

What is again overlooked is the fact that labor is not an abstraction, but living men, members of families, communities, residents of neighborhoods. All their normal drives are to sink roots, raise a family, enjoy friendly neighbors. With the exception of adventurous and restless individuals, migrations take place mainly when grave crises like wars, persistent unemployment, revolutions, and persecutions threaten people. When individuals not suffering such adversities move around excessively, we tend to regard them as casuals, or drifters. They are the men who occupy the waterfront, who make up the migratories of the harvest seasons. We frequently consider them a social problem. The personnel office in any company hesitates before putting such applicants on the payroll. They are the last to be hired, the first to be let go.

The truth of the matter is that the concept of mobility is a technical term in economics, an abstraction which gives value to a human being in terms of the market place, not in terms of the social life of a community. Is it consistent with the concept of community as a moral goal?

7

Who Is in "Politics"?

WE COME now to the implications of the traditional posture of businessmen toward unions and government, politics, and politicians.

Theoretically, businessmen on the whole are Jeffersonians in that they profess the belief that that government is the best which governs least. Accordingly, they stand for "nonintervention." They overlook the fact that under nonintervention government power is neutralized in favor of those who already possess economic power and privilege. It is those who feel weak in the market place, and on the whole disadvantaged, who agitate for government to do something positive for them to equalize their bargaining power.

In actual practice, however, hardly a business exists that does not want the government to do, or not to do, something for it. The textile industry wants a tariff, but merchants would like a free market to import cottons, silks, and woolens from all over the world.

Generally businessmen feel that what *they* ask of government is legitimate and in the interest of democracy. When, on the other hand, *labor* asks for social legislation, the same government becomes the "welfare state," or "creeping socialism." I confess to oversimplifying. Legitimate arguments may be made on one side or the other as to degree of government regulation. But it would serve the community better to admit frankly that government inevitably has to intervene in a thousand and one ways in this complicated world; it would be better to criticize specific measures in concrete terms, instead of whipping up propaganda clouds about the welfare state.

Welfare and Morality

It is well to pause on this matter of welfare; it goes to the heart of moral values. Concern for the welfare of our fellow man is basic in Judaeo-Christian teachings. It derives from the virtues of love and charity. Under the influence of propaganda, however, it has acquired invidious connotations. Hence the indictment of the "welfare state" as the road to serfdom.

Specifically, this attitude is revealed in opposition to social or protective legislation dealing with social security—unemployment, accidents, old age, sickness, and all the other characteristic hazards of industrial society—or legislation that legitimatizes trade unions such as the National Labor Relations Act. Here one must note that, traditionally, business has been against all these measures whether by local or Federal government and, whenever enactment seems inevitable, has initiated delaying tactics so as to reduce the scope of the particular law to as narrow coverage as possible.

Without going into the merits of any particular measure, one must hasten to say that it is well for businessmen to assume a critical attitude toward government action of this kind. Their role is to be prudent, to be conservative, to warn against overspending and bureaucratization of our economic and social life. But such an attitude is only one side of the argument.

Everywhere government is assuming greater responsibility for the hazards of industry and for the advancement of human welfare. Even businessmen have come around to thinking that it is beyond the capacity of any one company to assume these obligations. Although by the late 1930s government had made provisions for old age and unemployment, pensions and out-of-work benefits were quite low. It was only a matter of time before unions, when they felt strong enough, would make demands on corporations to bring such compensation to some sort of decent standard in relation to normal earnings. Thus in 1949 the late Philip Murray started this trend for supplementary pensions, and in 1955 Walter Reuther for supplementary unemployment compensation. It was then that corporate management began to take the position that all this was really a public responsibility and that existing laws should be so amended that the whole community, instead of an individual employer, should meet the cost of maintaining such expensive programs.

Management must be careful not so to misread the trend of history as to appear not conservative but reactionary. It should not always be "too late with too little." Supplementary compensation on a state and Federal level assuring nearly every citizen a minimum subsistence "from the cradle to the grave," although at one time anathema, has now won wide acceptance.

In former days, private charity and individual benevolence made some provision for the victims of economic hazards. But with the growth of the democratic idea, charity has become unpalatable. Social insurance offers a more comprehensive program, more certain of continuity, and it is less invidious because it is based on taxation rather than gifts of the rich to the poor. If human dignity is sacred, if a community with equality of opportunity is to prevail, then that community has the responsibility to provide maximum protection when economic life becomes so complicated and unstable that individuals themselves cannot save for contingencies.

People in Glass Houses

Businessmen frequently throw up their hands in despair, if not disgust, when they are dealing with union officials. They dismiss them as politicians.

To be sure, trade unions are to a large extent political organizations, and their leaders display the characteristics of politicians. They exaggerate their promises to their constituents. They know that they will never be able to deliver a fraction of the demands they make on management. They fulminate against heads of corporations as "greedy" men interested in profits at the cost of human welfare. For instance, John L. Lewis never fails at the proper state of a negotiation to ring the charges on "Wall Street" as pulling the strings behind the scenes to deny his miners their just deserts. Again, when the going gets rough, Walter Reuther usually challenges Henry Ford to debate with him in Briggs Stadium before the assembled multitude of Ford Motor Company employees the merits of the issues under negotiation. Ford always refuses this invitation to a "calm" discussion; so Reuther comes off as the "victor" by default.

Undoubtedly, union leaders perform as politicians. But are corporations free from politics, and do corporation executives never act as politicians? Of course they do. The only difference is that the two organizations and their leaders perform in a different political framework.

The trade-union official is elected by the rank and file. His mandate is a popular one, even though, as time goes on, he creates a political machine to assure his reelection. But no matter how strongly entrenched the machine may become, the growth of an opposition is not unknown, or even a revolt of the rank and file.

The corporation executive, on the other hand, is not elected by a mass vote. Indeed, his own employees have no voice in his appointment or retention. He is chosen by a board of directors and is responsible to them. He does not have to conduct any campaign against rivals. He is given a broad mandate to carry on and is fairly certain of being in office for his entire life. He may even determine his succession. He really occupies an authoritarian position at the will of the owners acting through the board of directors. Since his is an appointive office, he does not have to engage in politics, at least in the sense of swaying an electorate which directly and immediately controls his personal destiny.

At the same time, politics is a constant and normal activity characteristic of human society. We are all critical of the "seamy" aspects of politics. But the larger the electorate is, the greater are the emotional appeals, distortion, and demagogy. When corporation executives and their staffs attempt to secure mass support, they too appeal to emotions and distort their message, at times bordering on misrepresentation.

Thus in advertising, sales promotion, and merchandising, the businessman functions as a politician does: he appeals to the consumers for "votes" on behalf of his commodity or service —votes registered in sales. To be sure, standards of honesty and good taste have advanced considerably in recent years. Reputable business houses have themselves set up business bureaus in their respective communities to police fraudulent and misleading claims. Nevertheless, most of us react to the steady bombarding of competitive advertising almost in the same way as we do to the demagogy of politicians. Why do we have the term "huckstering"?

In truth, demagogy, distortion, and emotionalism are nothing less than a by-product of democracy, of freedom. Mankind has not yet grown up to that maturity responsive to rational appeals, to facts, to objective statements as to which is the best way to vote, the best commodity to buy, the best policy to support. This is an old story. It simply means that democracy has a long road ahead before it reaches the sophistication, the discrimination, the rationality, the good taste and morality, for which all of us yearn.

All to the Good

Even looking at politics in its more conventional sense, any businessman worth his salt tries to play his part in shaping public opinion and influencing political action along the lines he deems best. So do the United States Chamber of Commerce, the National Association of Manufacturers, and similar state and local associations. They represent business interests and naturally are continuously at work trying to influence legislators and executives at all levels of government to favor measures sponsored by them. In this sense, they try to do for business what the AFL-CIO tries to do for labor. Indeed, both have legitimate functions to discharge.

There are natural differences between one philosophy and another, between one school of economics and another, between one theory of political action and another. One believes in centralized, Federal action, the other in local state action; one believes in an active welfare program, the other in a minimum role for government. These are precisely the issues which go to make up politics.

Is it then a sound attitude, is it in the interest of community and communion, for management to indict unions and their leaders as "political," and so less than worthy of respect, and at the same time to exculpate business and its leaders from the "guilt" implicit in political activity?

So far America is the one major nation where political thinking has escaped contamination by the Marxian dogma which holds that historically society is divided into two classes—masters and slaves, lords and serfs, and currently into owners and proletariat—and that the class struggle is, therefore, inevitable and must culminate in a revolution in which the masses seize the means of production and distribution. To be sure, the Western democracies have themselves never adopted this theory completely. But even its modification in the form of the mild Fabian socialism of Britain or the democratic socialism of the Scandinavian nations, which eschews violence in favor of parliamentary gradualism, has never found fertile soil in this country—let alone the horror of Russian communism. This is something to be grateful for, as one of our many blessings.

But we must be careful to nourish the social and moral climate from which this immunity springs.

Management, of all groups, occupying as it does the controls of modern industry, bears a heavy responsibility in this regard. And, indeed, in recent years businessmen have developed a lively concern for the moral and ethical goals of industry. All the more one may urge, therefore, that they reexamine their attitude on strategic economic and political issues, to make sure that it does not lead, in however slight a measure, *toward* divisiveness, unhappiness, factionalism, aggression, and all the other characteristics of a sick society—and *away from* the sense of community which is so important a part of the Judaeo-Christian tradition and life as we know it in America.

PART III

The Danger of Cynicism

8

Cynicism and Managerial Morality

EARLIER in this book I noted the growing concern of businessmen with the ethical implications of their work. This, to me, is one of the heartening signs of our times. While science and secularism have undermined the influence of church and religion in so much of the community, businessmen have been struggling increasingly with the difficult task of squaring their function as wielders of economic power with the moral values of our Judaeo-Christian tradition. It is an exhilarating experience to see men engaged in the materialistic world of the market —in finance, production, selling, balancing profits and losses— so deeply involved in the moral issues of their workaday world.

Indeed, as one who moves in university circles, I am impressed with the greater concern with religious and moral values in business schools than among scholars in the humanities. The scholars are largely preoccupied not with substance but with technical scholarship—with the origin and evolution of ideas, with philological subtleties, with shades of meaning. Business schools, on the other hand, are faced continuously with the necessity of helping executives, in training and in practice, to make decisions involving the equities of employees, customers, government representatives, and trade-union officials. Almost always justice and fair dealing spring up as considerations, even though efficiency and profits are the explicit goals.

A personal experience brought this home to me: on reading some of this book, a noted scholar in the philosophy of religion turned and said to me, "You know, you write with moral fervor!" He did not mean this altogether as a compliment; to him, scholarship is technical and does not deal with values. By contrast, I feel—as do so many others—that one cannot study the tug of power between men and men, or between institutions and institutions, without becoming involved in ethical implications. Especially is this so in these critical days when naked power and its manipulation have been elevated to a major strategy in so many parts of the world, almost completely replacing old-fashioned diplomacy.

If teachers of business become thus involved, how much greater is the involvement of the practicing businessman. Living in an atmosphere of misunderstanding and even hostility, he is almost under the necessity to ponder ethical implications willy-nilly when making decisions. Indeed, this may constitute his major challenge: how to be efficient, make profit, *and* observe moral values. Elsewhere I have called this perpetual tension "the technical *must* versus the ethical *ought*." *

Roots of Cynicism

At the same time, however, one must also take note of a strain of cynicism in the business world amounting at times to a latter-day type of Machiavellism—especially in relation to government, trade unions, intellectuals, and even to difficult people within management's own plants, especially those who seem to thwart cherished objectives.

* See Sylvia Selekman and Benjamin Selekman, *Power and Morality in a Business Society*, McGraw-Hill Book Company, Inc., New York, 1956, part I, pp. 3–85.

Cynicism does not in itself completely identify this attitude. It also has elements of distrust, fear, and hostility. Surely it is not the quality of the "gentle cynic" who withdraws from life and laughs at the frailties of the human race. It is rather a pervasive suspicion that leads to questionable behavior, which in turn frequently boomerangs on business itself. For at times cynicism reaches the extreme of writing off all politicians and labor leaders as self-seeking, if not corrupt; and so it follows that the only practical recourse for management is to enter into deals, collusive arrangements, and backdoor agreements and to seek and retain the right "go-between." In the end all this frequently leads to the corruption exposed from time to time in the press. The revelations of the McClellan committee in 1957 and 1958 are a case in point.

How is one to reconcile cynicism with a simultaneous emphasis on moral values? Can it be that businessmen, smarting under long and severe attack, have now become so sure of their own rectitude that they look with contempt on those who do not go along with them? And if this is so, may it not follow that, unless executives come to grips with this drift toward cynicism and distrust, they are in danger of forfeiting whatever respect they have gained? One thing seems sure: they may as well face the fact that they will never again enjoy the opportunity for unilateral decision making. That day is gone forever. They must count on continuous opposition—and hopefully, as time goes by, on an intelligent, informed opposition—from the labor unions, farmers, consumer groups, reformers, and government agencies.

Another reason for this negative attitude may be that since so much of a modern executive's life is taken up with negotiation and bargaining, his path is bestrewn with temptation to take advantage of his superior economic position, as well as his greater knowledge, skill, and experience in the intimate matters of corporate life. Not infrequently he is under pressure to outsmart his opposite number in the union or a government agency, and he has a natural desire to outmaneuver any opponent who is trying to outsmart him. In fact, the temptation to get the jump on such an adversary is almost overwhelming.

Thus, cynicism finds in such a bargaining atmosphere a fertile soil in which to thrive.

Morality in Politics

Similarly, because bargaining and trading are such important aspects of politics, a cynical attitude prevails toward political activity. Indeed, by convention we tolerate a double standard of morality: a public posture on the highest moral level and a private life where deals and bargains are made. Since limits exist on the actual officeholders, it is the party leaders that really do the trading, the bargaining, and the making of deals. They raise the money necessary to keep the party going and frequently make implicit promises of preferment, or at least an inside track of good will with the administration, if and when it comes to office.

We leave politics to the "bosses." We shrug our shoulders as if to say, "What is the use?" And so an atmosphere of cynicism develops. Businessmen can hardly claim exemption from succumbing to this drift. Indeed, they have a ready excuse at hand; they have to be "practical." The argument seems to make so much sense that we may even look the other way when we see a leading executive noted for the highest integrity acquiescing in the behavior of a dubious, if not corrupt, politician for fear of reprisal against his own business interests. We forget—as probably he does—that in matters of character and morality, one cannot be cynical and moral at the same time. Once he takes a negative attitude toward human beings, it becomes difficult, if indeed not impossible, for him to inspire men with confidence in the integrity of his leadership.

9

Cynicism and Union Relationships

WHEN it comes to dealing with trade unions, fear intensifies cynicism. For a great many years corporations resisted and fought unions with every possible weapon—from influencing town and county officials to keep union organizers out as trespassers, to refusing unions permission to hold public meetings, arresting union leaders as disturbers of the peace, and finally to mobilizing special police or sheriffs with weapons to "shoot it out." Labor, too, has resorted to all kinds of dubious activity in trying to "reach" public officials, as well as in mobilizing its "military" forces. Again, cynicism easily becomes the natural attitude for justifying this kind of strategy.

During the late 1930s, most corporations finally realized that trade unionism could no longer be stood off. The acceptance of the inevitable was, however, mainly reluctant and, once again, cynical. The New Deal and Fair Deal were blamed, and Roosevelt, Perkins, and Truman were projected as the villains responsible for the invasion of property rights—the sit-downs, mass picketing, and other manifestations of raw power that accompanied the "explosion" in organizing activity.

Obviously, the new unions were bound to be crude and headstrong. Some of the leaders were dedicated men desiring to improve the lot of their fellow workers, but some were self-seeking, some corrupt, and some sympathetic with communism. It was bound to take time for these unions to make the transition from a fighting to an administrative stage and for the emergence of a leadership adequate to the requirements of newly acquired power and prestige. Indeed, serious problems of union administration still remain, as we shall examine later in this book.*

The temptation at the time was to try to make deals with those leaders considered "sensible," and/or to weaken and divide the unions and their leadership. In the prevailing climate, all this was understandable; recognition of unions did not come as a voluntary act, but rather as something imposed on company after company by economic and political power. Resentment and a latent desire to be punitive followed. Instead of realizing that what was called for was a long-range strategy founded on a sound moral basis, many managements let cynicism become their guiding philosophy. In so doing, they were sure to give hostage to conflict and hostility, and sometimes even corruption.

By playing Machiavelli one may think he assures himself the upper hand. He may even buy some immediate peace, or rather a semblance of peace. But only for a little while; the reckoning is sure to come.

To illustrate, after standing off the union for years in a no-quarter battle replete with violence, the Ford Motor Company rather "generously" agreed to put local union officials "on the payroll," so to speak, by agreeing to pay union committeemen or shop stewards average earnings for time spent in handling grievances. With Harry Bennett as key tactician, the company took a cynical, "if you can't beat them, join them" attitude. To this day, the Ford management, though raising the issue at each negotiation, has been unable to get out of that deal. And no wonder; it is hardly feasible for union officials, elected as they

* See Chaps. 24–26.

are by the very men involved, to agree to a change which would take away a "plum" from several hundred Ford employees.

Another illustration is afforded by General Motors Corporation. At the end of World War II, management did not have in its midst a "specialist" in making deals like Harry Bennett of Ford Motor Company, nor did its strategy call for such "talent." Instead, it followed the age-old, cynical, Machiavellian formula of "divide and rule." Stung by Walter P. Reuther's aggressiveness and militancy in the prolonged strike of 1945–1946, when he proposed a "look at the books," the management concluded negotiations first with the Communist-dominated United Electrical Workers (UE), though it did not represent nearly as many General Motors employees as did Reuther's United Auto Workers (UAW). However, James Matles of the UE and his fellow travelers "cooperated" eagerly with the General Motors management and agreed to a less costly "package" than that demanded by Reuther and the UAW. The Communist leaders were most anxious to cut their archenemy, Reuther, down to size. In fact, the UE and General Motors between them succeeded in leaving Reuther no other recourse but to follow along and accept the UE package for his union both in 1946 and 1947.

Thus, a major bastion of American capitalism played hand in hand with Communist "party liners"—both bent, though for different reasons, on preventing Reuther from rising to a place of power in the labor movement. Significantly, the settlement made in 1947 by General Motors and the UE became the pattern for the rest of the country. Indeed, it looked for a while as if the leading capitalist corporation and the leading Communist-dominated union would jointly become the dominant pattern-makers for American industry.

Need the lesson be pointed up? Cynicism and Machiavellism have a way of gnawing their corrosive course far past immediate tactics to eat away at such fundamental values as human freedom and dignity. Once the damage has been done, it takes almost a superhuman effort of the most intelligent management to make amends. For labor leaders and union members are also guilty of cynicism; they become more so when they hear corporations under these circumstances speak about the free enterprise system and the threat of communism to cherished liberties.

The last thing I wish to do is to rake up old coals. I refer to the Ford and General Motors episodes only to make us all the more aware of the natural temptations to yield to cynical stratagems. It is significant that both companies realized before long that such stratagems lead only to Pyrrhic victories and are self-destructive. For example, with the advent of Henry Ford II to leadership, the Ford Company soon rid itself of Harry Bennett. In 1949 it pioneered with the UAW in inaugurating a supplementary pension system and, in 1956, supplementary unemployment benefits, both of which became the patterns for industry. Again, by 1948, having been elected a second time to the presidency of the UAW, Reuther's leadership was recognized by General Motors as a fact that it was wise to accept, whether pleasant or unpleasant. Since then, negotiations between the company and the UAW have been characterized by an attempt to achieve some sort of realistic accommodation. Management broke new paths in 1948 by proposing that wages be based on the dual principle of increased productivity and fluctuations in the cost of living. Once the General Motors settlement was made with the UAW it became the pattern (by converting the wage formula to 13 cents an hour) for the rest of American industry, just as in the prior two years the agreement with the Communist-led UE had constituted the pattern.

The moral becomes obvious: corporations of the magnitude of Ford and General Motors let the whole nation down if they resort to cynical strategies, just as they break new paths for progressive stability when they follow ethical goals. In these matters as in personal relations, the larger and more powerful we are, the more we must look upon ourselves as "our brother's keeper." What is good for the country *must* be good for the great corporation.

Boulwareism

An outstanding example of cynicism is the managerial strategy represented by what has come to be known as Boulwareism, named after a General Electric vice-president, Lemuel R. Boulware. It is based on these principles:

1. Management knows best what should be done for its employees.
2. It should therefore make up its mind prior to any negotiation as to what should be the maximum offer.
3. It should refuse to recede from, or alter this offer in any substantial way.
4. It should take a strike, if necessary, and hold out until the union capitulates.

In a recent address,* Mr. Boulware severely indicted all unions without exception for using force instead of persuasion at the bargaining table, for developing a strategy of "political bargaining," and for "promoting the something-for-nothing, inflationary, foreign socialist brand of anti-business economics . . ." He called on businessmen to rally on the political field to defeat union leaders. He congratulated Arizona businessmen for having been active in the enactment of a "right-to-work" law, and told them that "a very important factor in General Electric's decision favoring Arizona over the other contenders for our Computor business was the combination of the fact that you *do* have a Right-to-Work law and the fact that a *growing majority* of the citizens are so obviously coming to appreciate and support voluntarism as opposed to compulsion in union membership."

Surely it is unfair to lump all unions under a blanket indictment. Corporations have suffered so much from such indis-

* L. R. Boulware, "Politics . . . the Businessman's Biggest Job in 1958," address before annual meeting, Phoenix Chamber of Commerce, Phoenix, Ariz., May 21, 1958.

criminate hate-mongering that it is difficult to understand a similar tactic by a spokesman for one of the country's leading corporations.

Under certain situations a strategy of containment may be a sound one—when dealing with a new and undisciplined union, or a Communist-dominated one, or one with irresponsible leaders, or if demands are so excessive as to threaten the company's competitive position. However, if the aim is to "cut a union down to size," to beat union leadership to the punch, then indeed the strategy is tantamount to a Machiavellian use of power to discredit, and, if possible, to destroy the union. It denies workers adequate and competent representation; for such tactics will never afford leaders an opportunity for development and growth. Indeed, the most serious moral defect of Boulwareism lies precisely in the fact that it deprives a human institution of the opportunity to grow in maturity and responsibility.

The labor movement is bound to take on increasing importance as time goes on. Although in the foreseeable future of this country we are not likely to face a labor party as do some nations in free Europe, trade unions and their adherents nevertheless play an important role in affairs of state as well as in industry. The best way for union members and leaders to acquire knowledge of the complex economic, political, and social factors at work is to learn through the negotiation and administration of agreements. But Boulwareism affords them little or no opportunity to undergo such an experience. It presents them with a "take it or leave it" ultimatum. The consequent danger may be a lethargic rank and file, with the radical, the impractical, or the militant rising to leadership; or, even worse, the corrupt and predatory may "muscle" in and take over. So we may face, if Boulwareism spreads, the risk of firmly established and powerful unionism without responsible membership and leadership—an ominous eventuality.

Joint Operation

Moreover, is it not a fallacy to assume, as does Boulwareism, that management can look out for employee welfare better than can union officials? In an age of specialization, management must have as its primary concern the economic health of the business as shown in profits; unions, the welfare of their members. The latter is not an easy job in a competitive world where industry must continually adjust to new technologies, shifting markets, or periods of recession, and where workmen must be transferred, furloughed, demoted, and even discharged.

In truth, modern industry is a combined operation for management and labor. It is arrogant for either group to assume that it has a key to superior wisdom or morality. They represent adverse as well as common interests. They may differ as to the distribution of proceeds; they agree on the desirability of maximum productivity. And everyone is the greater gainer when both mutual and conflicting interests are recognized and the parties gather around the table to negotiate the best possible agreement in terms of efficiency as well as of social justice.

Admittedly, the temptation to pursue the course of Boulwareism is strong. Labor leaders have to engage in a great deal of political maneuvering to get their members to accept settlements reached with management, and politics of this kind leads management to become impatient, if not cynical. They forget that union leaders, although they have behind them a political machine, must somehow meet expectancies which are often far beyond the realm of the possible. It takes adroitness to persuade union members who pay dues and elect officials to accept a smaller wage than they thought was "in the bag" during the prenegotiation campaign. Even as skilled and strong a leader as Reuther is confronted every once in a while with a "revolt."

One can easily become impatient when faced with the need of making commitments on cost and delivery while being kept in suspense by all this "politicking." How tempting it is to adopt Boulwareism as a strategy and thus be in a position to call the shots. Yet to do so is to imply a cynical attitude toward democracy and its capacity to develop sober, responsible leadership. In these human matters, as in strictly business ones, management must be willing to take risks.

Outside "Fixers"

It comes as a shock from time to time, to learn that a corporation of repute has betrayed its own standards of ethical behavior by accepting the standards of "fixers." What leads businessmen to enter into deals with men of questionable character in the hope of thus obtaining "peaceful" industrial relations?

The fall from grace usually has its beginning when a company, after successfully fending off a union, finally faces the necessity of coming to terms with it. It then turns to a lawyer or a consultant who "knows" his way about. The very act of turning to such a man is itself symptomatic of fear or cynicism, or both; and these attitudes are in danger of being sharpened as managers are exposed to the way the outsider "helps" them.

Admittedly, lawyers have an important role to play in the preparing for negotiations, in participating in the actual bargaining sessions, and in drafting the clauses of the final contract. But these are technical matters. In *policy making*, management must hew out its own course; it must take responsibility for ethical standards, strategy, and tactics. Counsel should be around only to help think through and carry out the policies decided on within the legal framework of state and nation. If the lawyer is closely identified with the management as a wise associate who has helped guide the corporation amidst the pressures of a changing world, well and good. There are many lawyers of this type who are real assets. But the vital decisions as to ethical standards, just as those involving costs and competition, should always remain with management.

What happens when management turns over too much responsibility to the lawyer and does not think through the problems for itself? An interesting example can come from the experience of a blue-chip company that was as outstanding for its product as for its public service. A strike had occurred in one of its plants. To take stock and avoid, if possible, the repetition of such shutdowns, a conference of central and plant personnel was called to which I was invited.

It turned out that a major problem was the weakness of the union. It had been proving a failure as a means of channeling employee attitudes to supervision, or of affording supervisors an avenue for discussing critical problems affecting productivity and employee morale.

It did not take long to discover the reason behind this failure. Among those present was the company's counsel. He dominated the discussion and always came up with a ready "simple" answer. Whenever one of his clients was subject to a union campaign, he said, he was usually called by labor leaders with the offer of a good "deal" if he would get the company to sign up for a union shop and the checkoff. These union leaders, he added, were primarily interested not in the men but in the "deals." He did not think that there was much hope in any effort to arouse interest in the union, which now enjoyed bargaining rights.

Later inquiry revealed that he was the very same lawyer who had brought this union in through a backdoor agreement with its president during the New Deal days when organizing campaigns were taking place all over the country.

Actually, it is not fair to put all of the blame on the lawyer. In the beginning, the company's management wanted a weak, compliant union. It failed to see that this was at best a short-lived expedient. All sorts of problems began arising daily in its various plants which involved employee relationships, but local executives had no one with whom to discuss them. The union president who had made the deal was located far from any of the plants, and knew little about what was going on.

To management's credit, it realized that its previous course of action had not been paying off and it commenced working on a more realistic approach. It realized that once a union comes into a plant, it is to the interest of management to have it active. Otherwise, supervisors have no one with whom to handle the problems which are bound to arise from day to day.

"Hiring Away" Union Officials

Another aspect of cynicism is to tempt into the management fold the man who shows ability and aggressiveness as a union official. "Why not put this man on our side," executives may say. "If he is good enough for the union, he ought to be good enough for us."

Such thinking fails to take into consideration the consequences of depriving a union of leadership. To hire away an effective union official is to create a vacuum. A less able person is likely to be elected as successor; the men may flounder around without anyone to guide them through the maze of economic, technical, and social problems that inevitably arise from day to day. And so again management finds itself baffled because of lack of adequate representation of its employees.

Another point overlooked frequently is that the transition from one role to another, in which a man virtually changes sides, is fraught with the danger of misunderstanding and suspicion. He runs the risk of being suspected of being a turncoat —for money. And if (as it often happens) he is appointed to a position in personnel, in which as the administrator of managerial policies he may have to take positions contrary to the very ones he fought for in his union role, then the potential damage to confidence in the integrity of management is great.

This is not to say that an employee who becomes active in union affairs should never be promoted to a managerial position. But the move should be made only after full discussion. If management then favors it still, care should be taken in the early stages not to put the erstwhile union official in a position where he has to oppose the very union which he has left, such as leading the management in negotiating a new contract, or representing it in an arbitration procedure, or acting as a witness against his former brethren. Of course, the temptation is overwhelming to do that very thing—to turn over to the former labor official the job of making his erstwhile brethren "reasonable." To give in to it, however, is to impart to the people inside and outside of the plant an underlying attitude of cynicism.

A related form of temptation—equally important to resist—is the hiring of a local celebrity or politician as personnel or labor relations director. The elevation of Harry Bennett by the elder Henry Ford is an extreme example. To be sure, an ex-mayor or other former public office-holder may know how to manipulate and "fix" troublesome officials in government or in the union. But whether or not bribes are passed (very often they are not), the reputation of the company becomes blemished as the suspicion spreads, not only inside the mill gates but also throughout the entire community.

10

Cynicism, Justice, and Equity

FREQUENTLY one finds a management cynical not only in over-all dealings with unions but also in the handling of individual cases, particularly when settlements made in the front office are not accepted at the shop level. Such behavior provokes executives to comment that the union men cannot be trusted, that they are "just politicians," whereas the truth of the matter is that frequently the difficulties inherent in the human situation are of a dimension not easily disposed of by a "settlement."

Here, from a case I became familiar with several years ago, is the kind of thing that can happen when one man is treated in a way which his fellow workers consider unjust: a veteran employee whom I shall call Andy was an all-round welder who could work with electric, acetylene, and other tools. He had worked for the company for about thirty years. In his early years, when welding was not nearly as extensively used as now, he had helped train novices in the job. Over the years, indeed, Andy had always received the highest incentive rate.

During the war, when welding superseded riveting, the company decided, with the consent of the union, to develop a job classification plan for welders. Andy felt, as did his "buddies," that he would always get the highest rate, no matter what new jobs arose; in fact, he thought that management had made such a promise to him.

Subsequent to the completion of job classification, however, two higher rates were established to cover welding on heavy construction outside the shop. Andy continued to remain *in* the shop, where he had always been, and complained that he suffered an injustice in the form of a wage cut.

When his grievance could not be adjusted in the department, it went to top executives at the plant level and the corresponding union officials. There a settlement was reached. The company agreed to pay Andy the difference between what he had earned and what he would have earned had he gone out on the construction jobs even though management could find no one who remembered promising him the highest rate. The difference for fifteen months amounted to $60. Andy was sent a check with the understanding that the grievance was settled; henceforth, if he wished, he could continue to earn the highest wage by taking on the jobs outside the shop.

But was the grievance settled? Not by a long shot! In fact, it was finally appealed to arbitration. Both company and union had failed to understand that the insignificant amount of $60 did not touch the heart of the matter. Worker after worker protested that Andy had been wronged, that he was entitled to, and should receive, the highest rate. They spoke of him as a responsible leader both for them and the company. It was a disgrace, they insisted, to demote him now—yes, to "degrade" him.

Management admitted that at one time Andy constituted a "one-man" department but argued that the company now had a diversified crew and any number of welders to turn to for whatever work might be needed. Andy *could* still earn the highest rate if he would go out and work on heavy construction jobs, management pointed out.

Since Andy insisted on remaining in the shop, he had really become little more than what the company classified as a "handy man," handing out glass and rods to the welders. The appellation of "handy man" outraged other workers. They charged that the company was discarding a valuable old employee after having gotten the best out of him for years. Did not management realize that, as a teacher, Andy always stayed in the shop? That was where he was expected to be for whatever emergency might arise. To expect him now in his late years to climb construction trestles was shameful.

Thus, the settlement made in the front office by top company and union officials had been rejected at the shop level because, in the eyes of the ranks, a cynical evaluation had been placed on Andy and his contribution over the years.

The union officials next found themselves in an embarrassing dilemma when they failed to get the rank and file to accept their settlement with management. So they, too, resorted to a questionable stratagem. They now argued that the foreman and superintendent were showing hostility to, and discriminating against, Andy because he had complained, that the agreement was therefore not being carried out in good faith. This effort to reopen the case made managers all the more cynical; they now were quite sure that the union representatives were not trustworthy.

Thus cynicism finally destroyed a natural foundation for strengthening morality. Instead of building a richer relationship on the human values which surrounded Andy and his fellow welders, and thus elevating the technical importance of welding to the moral heights of a "guild," the episode ended in bitterness and frustration. Those who were cynical became more so, and those (particularly the riveters) who had started out with good will ended up distrusting both company and union.

Old Workers on New Jobs

A note of impatience merging into snideness not infrequently creeps into discussions relating to older employees.

I have sat at meetings where plant executives threw their hands up, baffled as to what to do with older employees, once skilled and valued men but no longer up to handling newer, more complicated tools and processes. As long as manual skill and judgment are the chief requirement, they are "tops." But when, with increasing mechanization, it comes to handling complex continuous processes with close tolerances, their responses are no longer flexible enough. The foreman or engineer has to stand by to step into the breach when anything goes wrong.

Beyond physical factors, one confronts here what is undoubtedly a major psychological difficulty—whether an older man of skill and craftsmanship can ever adjust himself to increasing automation, indeed, whether he ever really accepts it. Nevertheless, if management truly means what it says when it talks about human dignity as basic in American morality, it surely cannot afford to look down its nose at highly valued men who made their contribution in their time to the growth of a business.

To be sure, local plant managers are often on the spot. Maximum productivity is expected from new equipment in which large capital investments have been made. If they fail, plant executives are called to task. They are thus caught between the human problems of the older people and the "hardheaded" pressures of top management. Obviously the balance of power is on the side of the latter.

It is therefore only natural to become impatient with the difficulties of older workers. From impatience it is but a step to cynicism. They are mentioned with condescension. They are moved from job to job until they become handy men with lower status and less pay. What is overlooked is the impact of such treatment on the plant community. Since reverence for the aged is a Judaeo-Christian virtue, one which is all the more observed if the elders have in their time made a contribution to the life of the community, any management that handles a middle-aged employee even remotely in a spirit of cynicism thereby forfeits respect for itself.

Justification for Discipline

An underlying cynical attitude leads at times to excessively harsh discipline, justified, if challenged, by a spurious mixture of technical and moral arguments. For example, an employee holding the highest position in his department was demoted three rungs, ostensibly for failure to observe the rule of notifying his foreman at home when a breakdown occurred. The demotion was so drastic as to obviate any possibility of even a temporary reassignment to the highest post if, on any day, the new incumbent failed to turn up.

The case was appealed to arbitration. Management argued that the breakdown and loss of production was not the only reason for the demotion. In the past, he had failed both to observe safety regulations and also to maintain harmony among his crew.

The clear and undisputed fact was that not until the event of the breakdown and the consequent loss of production was the severe penalty imposed. No regard was given to the man's long service, stretching over thirty years, nor to the fact that he had served in the top job for nine years and supervised a crew of a dozen men operating complicated machine tools, nor to the fact that he was one of the highest production men in the mill. Clearly he was without malice or ill will to his men or the company. He was almost naïve as he expressed "love" for his job.

Indeed, if any fault was to be found, it was his overzealousness for production, which led him to drive his men and occasionally to neglect safety regulations. But it should not have been overlooked that the prevailing incentive system put all the emphasis on production: the greater the output, the higher the take-home pay.

What bothered me most about the case was that at the hearing management based its defense primarily on a lofty "human relations" argument that the man had failed to secure a co-operative spirit in his crew, and, on occasion, had jeopardized their lives and limbs.

To use a moral argument to justify a questionable demotion precipitated by a costly failure in production evidenced, to my way of thinking, a cynical attitude—cynical toward the employee as well as toward the arbitration process. No one seriously believed that the man had willfully failed to observe the rules of decent human conduct; the only issue was a purely materialistic one—the cost of a machine breakdown.

As a matter of fact, though my award called for his reinstatement, so acute was his humiliation and sense of injustice that before long he quit.

Use of Technicalities

An underlying attitude of cynicism is also, I believe, responsible for an overlegalistic handling of human situations at the sacrifice of individual equity. Let me illustrate with two grievance cases in one plant: In the first case, a machinist was allowed to take Wednesday and Thursday off one week in lieu of part of his regular vacation; color photography was his hobby, and he wanted to take pictures of a flower show that was in town. He returned to work on Friday.

Normally Saturday was a day off; when worked, it was paid at overtime. The machinist came to work Saturday at the request of his foreman, who signed his time card crediting him with time and a half. His paycheck included the extra money for that day. Shortly thereafter, however, the auditors ran across this item, judged it an overpayment because the man had not worked the five previous days, as stipulated under the union agreement, and deducted it from his next paycheck.

This case happened during a period of full employment, when a skilled man could easily pick up a job on Saturday at a premium rate. The machinist came into work to help out his foreman, and both understood that overtime would be paid. In fact, after the deduction had been made, the foreman went to the management and urged that it be restored. Management, however, refused. It became a grievance, and eventually went to arbitration. It appeared that the company was not so much concerned with the money involved (under $10) as with the formal legalism of the contract and the danger of establishing a precedent. In its desire to press a technical advantage, instead of making an exception, it overlooked the equities of the machinist as well as the relationship between him and the foreman.

In the second case, management had allowed a fitter a make-up rate on special-order work, which consumed about half of his time. This practice virtually guaranteed a minimum day rate when working on nonincentive jobs. Again, an alert auditor scanning the payroll concluded that, under the contract negotiated five years earlier, it was not necessary to pay any make-up or special rates; in fact the practice was prohibited.

As of a certain date, therefore, management stopped paying the fitter his extra bonus. The result was that he lost, on the average, about 15 cents an hour every day in comparison with his usual incentive wages. Management made no attempt to work out an incentive rate for the special work (it maintained it could not be done), or to find some other legalistic formula by means of which it could continue the customary practice of paying this man his average incentive earnings (legalism *can* be made to work toward, as well as away from, equity).

It turned out that the fitter was the only one in the crew skilled enough to do what amounted to a tailored job on joints required for bridges and other types of construction. Thus in a sense he was doing management a favor by taking on these assignments. Under the circumstances both he and his friends were deeply offended that instead of a reward, he should actually suffer a loss. But the argument of the company was that just because it had paid "an extra bonus" to this man for five years was no reason why it should continue to "overpay" him. Should it be penalized, it asked blandly at the arbitration hearing, for either "carelessness" or "generosity" up to this time?

The sense of injustice became all the more acute when the company interposed a technical, procedural bar to my decision on the merits of the case. It argued that arbitration was barred on the ground of "untimeliness." The union had failed to appeal the case to arbitration within the time limits specified in the contract. This had happened because of the inexperience of the full-time union official who was new on his job; this was the first time he had ever invoked arbitration. He had thought the minutes of the prior joint grievance meeting, as recorded by the company, in error and returned them for correction. He was of the opinion that he could still appeal to arbitration after the parties had agreed to the correctness of the record. He was wrong; the wording of the contract was clear. But it was an error growing out of inexperience.

The importance of upholding the procedural aspects of law is not to be denied. But obviously one has to use discrimination. Where equities are so compelling, as in the case of the machinist and the fitter, and when inexperience accounted for the lapse in the procedure of appealing his case, to press a legal advantage which would shut off even consideration of merits was tantamount to depriving the situation of all moral value.

As arbitrator in these two cases, I found for the men, frankly basing my award on the equities of the case, though the literal wording of the agreements upheld management. Even though I went out of my way to make it clear that I was making an exception which was not to be considered a precedent, I received a withering letter from the company protesting that my decision exemplified a double standard of conduct: one for the company, and one for the union!

In another situation, though upholding management, I expressed sympathy for an employee who had been discharged. He had been engaged on a finishing process; acceptance or rejection of the product depended largely on the quality of the finish. This man's eyes became weak and his eyesight more and more impaired. Having worked twenty years for the company, he was offered treatment by an ophthalmologist and glasses—all at company expense. But the man was a health faddist and refused. Nature's remedies were the best: he drank fruit and vegetable juice and exercised his eyes.

It looked downright silly for a middle-aged man to forfeit a good job by refusing medical aid to correct a physical defect. And yet here was an intelligent man who was doing just that. And so even though I found against him, I expressed regret that no other place was available where he might work despite his impaired eyesight; hence I had no alternative but to sustain his discharge.

Later I visited another company. I was greeted with the statement, "How could you find the way you did? My dear professor (you are called 'professor' when you are taken down a peg!), when will you learn that a business is not an eleemosynary institution?" I asked, "Did you read all the facts? Was not the man entitled to some sympathy when cast out from a community in which he had served acceptably for twenty years?" The only reply was a cynical smile.

11

Cynicism and Intellectuals

ONE of the most serious manifestations of cynicism is the attitude of distrust toward "intellectuals," especially toward the unorthodox and the nonconformist. The intellectual may be no more radical than Professor (now Justice) Felix Frankfurter, but rather an "old-fashioned" liberal in the Holmes and Brandeis tradition. If, however, he advised and assisted in shaping something that was called a New Deal program, or was moved earlier to challenge the ways of justice as meted out to two immigrant Italians, he is in danger of losing his standing as the result of the battering of influential alumni, many of them businessmen.

The shrieks of intolerance are all the more strident if a teacher or scientist was naïve enough, in the flush of youthful idealism, to join anything like a Communist cell, or just to attend meetings where Communists congregated.

Indeed, the attitude of many businessmen toward the intellectual is contradictory, if not almost pathological. On one hand, corporations welcome eagerly the findings of scholars which contribute to technological advance or to a better understanding of human behavior. On the other hand, in their rejection of the intellectuals, businessmen create a hostile climate and thus undermine the very creativity essential for a progressive technology and improved human relations. They forget that when things are new and in a pioneering stage, theories and findings may sound offensive and even shocking. People do not like to be disturbed from their familiar moorings, whether they be physical, social, or intellectual. The story of Galileo is an oft-told tale, but, alas, each generation forgets it.

Admittedly, the intellectual often exposes himself to attack, especially when he enters the public arena and criticizes those in authority in areas beyond his technical competence in his own specialty. Such individuals should be exposed for their error or naïvete in the open forum of public debate. Can we, however, afford to generate a hostile atmosphere against *all* intellectuals in face of the cataclysm hovering over mankind? Indeed, even if we surmount the present danger, the only wealth and power that counts in the end, for peace as for war, is that derived from the intellectual capital accumulated by scholarship in science and the humanities. To maintain, under such circumstances, a distrustful and cynical attitude toward scholars is to cut the very ground from under the most creative men.

Beyond the current crisis is the long-range challenge of coming to grips with the destructive potential in man: his capacity for hate like that for love, for evil as for good. For this purpose, too, we must turn to our scholars in the social and medical sciences, in the humanities, and in the theological seminaries in order to keep revitalizing and enriching the intellectual, moral, and aesthetic resources of mankind to sustain and guide us through our perplexities.

12

Cynicism and Executive Authority

MUCH has been said and written about the sources of authority that give management the sanctions to direct men. It has long since been recognized that authority based on rights of property, though controlling in courts of law, carries little weight in the daily life of a corporation. Thus it has become fashionable to say that authority comes, not from above, but "from below."

But what is it that comes "from below"? The most potent factor, I submit, is the moral atmosphere projected by the chief executive and his management group. No one can exercise power effectively these days without conveying the conviction that he does so responsibly, that is, with justice. Since management combines in itself the usual three functions of government—legislative, executive, judiciary—and since it is self-perpetuating, it constitutes a tremendous holder of power.

Because of our democratic, Judaeo-Christian society, the legality of property rights must give way to consent. But how does one obtain consent? By the conviction that power is controlled by, and directed toward, ethical goals. It is not the words that are important. It is attitude and behavior that convey the omnipresence of a moral posture. In this sense, authority does not come from below but rather stems from the integrity of the entire business as a human institution fraught with moral values.

A cynical attitude is in direct contradiction to all this. Indeed, by definition it implies distrust of human motives; it is bound to breed suspicion. And so individuals, be they supervisors, technicians, or hourly workers, do not feel comfortable with a cynical leader. The only recourse then available to the executive is to use power in the form of fear and intimidation.

For a while, during the nineteenth and early twentieth centuries, fear may have been effective; the industrial scene was influenced by such conditions as surplus labor, mass immigration, and nothing but private charity between work and starvation. In recent years, however, a host of protective agencies has sprung up to prevent arbitrary discipline or discharge and to provide maintenance on at least a modest level until another job is obtained. Even more, the whole moral and social climate has so changed that no longer can a "boss" govern for any length of time by threats of punishment. Thus, from a practical point of view, since management cannot rule by force, cynicism destroys the main sanction for authority, for it undermines man's faith in man.

If anyone thinks I am overly idealistic, let him recall the "big" men he has worked under. Was it not confidence in their sense of justice and fair play as well as in their technical ability that made them the leaders they became in their respective industries and communities? Moreover, if it be true that the contemporary crisis of society is a moral one, that men are losing faith in the old ways of doing things and turning more and more to powerful politicians; if it be true that man is trying to escape from freedom into the arms of all-powerful government, what alternative is there but to generate the faith that rises from a morally responsible attitude in the everyday exercise of authority?

Cynicism erodes inner strength. If one is to handle large and complex responsibilities, as do most business executives, one has to be fortified by belief in the people who surround him.

One does not receive confidence unless he gives it to others. It is these imponderable elements that give vitality to an institution as a living community of men, that call forth effort beyond the line of duty, and that make one want to excel in all things.

Unless checked, cynicism may destroy whatever faith people may be developing in the integrity of bankers, manufacturers, merchants, and other business groups in their respective communities. It may isolate the centers of a moral renaissance and abort the efforts of leaders to raise the social consciousness of management. Cynicism is negation. To the cynic, man is basically and always selfish, self-aggrandizing, and exploitative of his fellow man. Surely this is completely contrary to what thoughtful businessmen assume about human nature when they emphasize social and ethical goals.

All this is not without significance in the contemporary, world-wide crisis. Let us remember that the Communist imperialists condemn capitalist democracy as doomed precisely because it is inherently cynical, selfish, and exploitative. Surely, as we reach out for friends and allies, we can ill afford to play into the hands of our enemies. And within the nation, it is well to put our house in order.

PART IV

The Danger of Perfectionism

13

Sin Bravely: The Danger of Overcommitment

God does not save those who are spurious sinners (but real sinners). Be therefore a sinner and sin bravely, but all the more have trust and rejoice in Christ who is the victor over sin and death and the world.

Martin Luther

Of course Luther did not mean to encourage sin. Rather was he bent on making man aware of his human estate—his fallibility, his imperfections. Indeed, in underscoring his doctrine of salvation by faith, Luther sought to comfort man with the thought that, though he could never attain unto perfection, he must nevertheless not despair but rejoice in the grace that enables him to aspire.*

Long before Luther, the Hebrew sages of the Talmud similarly warned, "The Law was not given to angels." † The point again was that, though complete insight may never be attained, man

* The full text follows: "Deus non facit salvos ficte peccatores. Esto peccator et pecca fortiter, sed fortius fide et gaude in Christo, qui victor est peccati, mortis et munde." *Dr. Martin Luthers Werke,* Böhlau, Weimar, 1883–1948; Briefwechsel, 2. Band, 1931, p. 372.

† Babylonian Talmud, Berakoth 25b.

should not become discouraged but seek rather to find fulfillment in the persistent effort to understand God's word.

Danger of Overcommitment

It is well for businessmen and those engaged in the rapidly growing profession of management to keep these admonitions in mind. Indeed, my purpose in referring to Luther and the Talmud is not so much to bring comfort as to warn. I fear that spokesmen for American industry may be in danger of giving an impression of managerial competence not warranted by the present state of knowledge and of making commitments to ethical standards impractical of realization.

To be more specific, let me illustrate by a personal experience: twice I have found it necessary during the past year to apologize to policy-making businessmen for not being able to perform "miracles." In each case it seemed to be tacitly assumed that modern concepts of business and tools for diagnosing management problems enabled one to have almost magical powers.

The occasions were meetings with managerial groups of two companies which had invited me to advise with them. In the first instance, I was given two weeks to visit the corporate headquarters, three regional offices, and three operating plants widely distributed in three different states. Indeed only the "air age" —and company planes—made such coverage possible. In the second instance, I came at seven o'clock one evening in time for dinner and left before dinner the following evening. I spent the day listening to headquarters people and plant managers from some dozen installations report about their problems.

These were not routine visits to observe routine matters. One company asked me for an evaluation of its labor relations policies. A wage negotiation was pending as the result of an industry-wide movement; the usual tensions and uncertainties attending such bargaining in these days of inflation were in the air. In the other company, a strike had taken place in one of the plants—an entirely unexpected strike, which had shaken everyone. It was for that reason that I was invited. Management wanted to do everything possible to prevent a recurrence of such a shutdown, as well as to take stock generally and chart out any modifications in policy in the handling of employee and union relations.

Among my audience in both companies were not only men dealing with production, sales, control and finance, but also, as might be expected in growth industries, those engaged in research in the physical sciences, pure and applied—chemists, physicists, geologists, metallurgists, and engineers. *Both* groups of men expected me to be able to give them an authoritative evaluation of how their company was functioning, in spite of the completely inadequate time allotted for my observations.

And so I took occasion to contrast the materials and methods available in the physical sciences with those available in the social or behavioral sciences, and both sets of techniques with the entirely empirical method of management. In one of the companies the meeting took place in the conference room of the science laboratories, which gave me an unusual opportunity to make vivid the relative uncertainty and tentativeness of the disciplines dealing with human behavior as compared with the certitudes of the physical sciences.

I begged my audience not to think of me as a "charlatan." I protested that I would have to spend considerable time—perhaps a year—with a team of colleagues before I could render an authoritative report on so dynamic an aspect of their operations as labor relations and human relations. (Some of the personality problems alone, as revealed by the symptoms reported by plant executives, would have taken psychiatrists months to study, let alone treat.) I went on to say that all I could give were the tentative impressions of an experienced observer, which I assumed was all they expected of me at this stage.

I narrate this experience not because of my own perplexity, but to put management's responsibilities in proper perspective.

The very fact that companies of such stature could expect me to perform a "miracle" in so brief a time underscores the dangers besetting the rapidly growing profession of management. Indeed, I am deeply concerned lest management assume too great a burden in giving the impression that it can do thoroughly and well all the tasks it is undertaking. And by the same token, I fear that the community may be in for grave disappointment unless the limitations of management are understood. One of these days, business may have another experience of being projected as a scapegoat for recession and unemployment, or whatever crisis may overtake the community.

For in the effort to counter communist propaganda, American businessmen have been giving an impression of a capability which may prove difficult to live up to. I do not mean to imply for one moment that our own industrial organization as a whole is not superior to that of Russia. But we must be careful to conserve the vitality that goes with the freedom and initiative characteristic of our system. To do so we must not put too great a burden upon those men who are responsible for the conduct of industrial enterprise. Nor must we, regardless of how lofty our aspirations, set our sights so high as to be beyond the achievable in the here and now. For instability in the form of inflation, deflation, prosperity, recession, and much personal hardship is one of the prices, heavy as it is, that apparently we must pay in our present state of knowledge for the precious assets of freedom and creativity inherent in our decentralized industrial system.

14

Limitations of Managerial Tools

PERHAPS what I have in mind may become clearer if we try to put industrial management in perspective with other professions.

I think it accurate to say that the manager of an industrial enterprise is nothing less than a combination of practicing social scientist and artist. As such, his effectiveness must depend to a large extent on the materials furnished by the social sciences as well as by the art of administration.

One outstanding characteristic differentiates him from the pure scientist: he cannot be content just with the observation and recording of his findings; he must act. His responsibility is to see that things get done, whereas that of the scientist is to observe accurately and to report on his observations with as much generalization as he deems feasible. His responsibility ends with his report.

Another characteristic distinguishes the manager from the artist: in creating products and services he must keep his public constantly in mind. By contrast, the artist, for his part, is not responsible for any action involving people. All he has to do is to write, paint, sculpt, or compose that which expresses what he thinks and feels. He may be as indifferent as he pleases to his audience. In all probability the better the artist, the less will he compromise with public taste. But in business, public taste must be constantly considered; and although the artist may be criticized when he yields to public taste, the business executive may not survive unless he does. He has to work with other people's capital, other people's labor, and other people's materials. He has to cater to other people's tastes. Unless he is able to pay his way and turn all this into a profit, he will not attract any of these groups and their respective contributions. Sooner or later he will have to shut down his shop.

Inadequate Tools

Yet at times it would seem, judging from the expectations aroused in the minds of the community, that the business executive has at his command the tools and methods of the scientist, the perception and craftsmanship of the artist —and beyond these, the cunning of Satan and the wisdom of the Lord. To a large extent management itself is responsible for this dilemma. Typically it takes the position these days that it does not represent any one group, neither labor nor capital, nor the consumer, nor the supplier of raw and semifinished materials; instead it acts as coordinator and, as such, tries to balance the equity of all these strategic groups.

It is true, of course, that the modern manager is no longer the owner of the business as was the employer-manager a generation ago, that he is engaged by a board of directors who have evaluated his competence and character to conduct a business successfully, and that he is likely to be a graduate of a school of business. Thus, in many ways management takes on a professional aspect, as does any group specially trained for a job. But both training and materials are still experimental, and very far from exact. Indeed, the basic materials available to management on planning, control, industrial relations, and so on, are less well developed than those at hand, let us say, for teaching, let alone such well-established professions as medicine, law, and engineering.

And yet the responsibilities of the manager are more varied, more complex, and more difficult than those of most other professionals. He must know how to raise the capital needed for the enterprise—whether to float long- or short-term bonds and stocks, or whether to borrow one way or another from banks or insurance companies. He must know production in its latest technical aspects: materials, machines, factory layout, location, proximity to raw materials, labor, markets, and the rest. He must know accounting, how to estimate his costs, and how to price his product.

He must know how to market his product through the whole complex of advertising, distribution agencies, and retail outlets. He must be aware of shifts of consumer demand with regard to quality, style, and price. He must know how to deal with unions so as to obtain efficient labor at a cost that will enable him to compete. He must know something about government regulations and their impact upon his business. These days he must also be a public educator interpreting to the community not only his own business but the function of business as a whole in the modern world.

Finally, since he cannot do all these things himself, the modern corporation executive must know how to build an organization. He must choose individuals with ideas, skill, and initiative and yet forge them into cooperative teams. In short, he should have the qualifications of an educator and leader tailored to the specific needs of a business organization. Indeed, it is in this respect that administration becomes an art.

Social Scientist

To put all the foregoing in terms of modern disciplines, the corporation leader must be an economist, psychologist, political scientist, sociologist, and anthropologist as well as a businessman with a good working knowledge of statistics, accounting, production, engineering, marketing, and the other specialized activities employed in the daily conduct of a business enterprise. In effect, therefore, he is a practicing social scientist, a clinician.

He is a psychologist because he deals with human behavior, both as manifested in individuals and groups. Indeed, he should know something about abnormal psychology; unless he is unusually fortunate, he cannot escape having a certain proportion of neurotics in his organization—both at executive and nonsupervisory levels—maladjusted men with unhappy family lives. He must be a political scientist, for essentially he is a governor of men; he handles power with, and over, others within his organization, as well as in opposition to the power of external groups represented by trade unions and government agencies. He certainly must be acquainted with the economics of his industry and know how to interpret economic trends in the country as a whole. He must have some acquaintance with sociology and anthropology, with the way people organize themselves into groups; he must be sensitive to the emotions, sentiments, and ideas that underlie conflict as well as cooperation.

Trial and Error

But what is the state of development of the behavioral sciences? What tools do they yield which management may use to discharge its manifold, complex responsibilities? Certainly there has been very heartening progress during the past fifty years or so; yet a brief review of these questions will, I believe, serve as a sobering reminder of the limitations that management works under.

The one discipline which impinges on managerial action as a technical activity more than any other is economics. As financier, as producer, as purchaser, and as distributor, the modern businessman is constantly confronted with economic problems; he operates an economic system within the larger system of the total economy, and there is, of course, a large degree of interdependency between the two.

But the methods of economics as a discipline, although interesting and intellectually challenging, are hardly of a nature to assist the business executive in his daily task of making strategic decisions on what to make, how to price and market, whether to build up or reduce inventories, and so forth. Both method and conclusions are quite theoretical, and based on "models"—that is to say, artificial situations—rather than on actual problems.

Moreover, the increasing tendency to employ mathematics as the language of analysis renders the subject inaccessible to the practical business administrator. Indeed, the latest developments in economics make the material and thinking available in large part only to specialists; economics has developed a dialectic all its own which only the professional initiates can understand and use as a method of communication.

Of course, popularizations are available for the businessman, as are a variety of economic services which cater to industry. But at best they offer essentially background material to help him think through problems with greater sophistication, to weigh alternatives, to decide which course of action may carry a lesser risk. On the whole, it would not be an exaggeration to say that if executives had to rely heavily on going economic theory, they would be unable to make decisions on most of the matters of policy which come before them.

Even on matters of broad policy, economics can offer only a range of advice; there are too many differences among economists and their respective schools of thought. One has only to ponder the problem of gradual inflation which has confronted the country during the postwar years to appreciate how great these differences are. Or take the business recession in 1958, with its accompanying unemployment. Men of good will and equal standing as competent economists gave diagnoses and prescriptions with regard to the recession of 1958 ranging all the way from a minimum of Federal interference to a comprehensive program of tax reduction, public works, acceleration of defense spending, enlarged and extended unemployment relief, and so on.

And so, no matter how much he may want to rely on economics, the executive is left with the responsibility of making his own decisions as best he may. I do not wish to minimize the importance of a knowledge of economic forces in helping to reach judgments. My point is simply that economics makes no tools available for the managerial executive comparable even in the smallest degree to those which, let us say, medical science affords the physician.

Latitudes of Accounting

Of all the disciplines, accounting is perhaps the most basic for management. It is the language system of business. By means of it an executive has a check on the health and vitality of his organization. Do his decisions result in a product or service which the consumer wants at the price decided upon? Is the company paying its way? Does this price yield enough to pay for capital, tools, raw and semifinished materials, labor, depreciation, and enough profit to assure the continuity of the business?

Accounting is the most accurate and rigorous of all the disciplines available to industry. Figures take the place of guesswork. Yet it comes as a surprise, if not a shock, to anyone not close to industry to learn how reluctant accountants are to give the impression that they can give a completely accurate account of how a business is doing. Thus, according to the late Marquis G. Eaton, speaking as president of the American Institute of Certified Public Accountants: "Accounting is not a natural science but a social science. It measures and communicates information about economic activities, which, because they involve human motivations and judgments, are themselves dynamic and unstable." He cautions the ordinary reader against thinking that there exists "some authoritative code of accounting, which when applied consistently will produce precise and comparable results." He warns us against the impression that the phrase, "generally accepted accounting principles," with which auditors conclude their reports, constitutes a clearly defined comprehensive set of rules which will ensure identical accounting treatment of the same kind of transaction in every case.

Thus, in inventory evaluation, the last in, first out method will show less net income in a period of rising prices than the first in, first out method. Again, "a company which adopts the diminishing balance method of depreciation may show less income in the early years and a greater net income in the later years of the life of the given assets than an identical company which follows a straight method of depreciation."

He concludes: *

> It no doubt comes as a shock for some people to realize that two otherwise identical corporations might report net income differing by millions of dollars simply because they follow different accounting methods and that the financial statements of both companies might still carry a certified public accountant's opinion stating that the report fairly represented the results in accordance with "generally accepted accounting principles."

Uncertainties of Marketing

If this be true of accounting, which is the most exact and rigorous of all tools of business administration, what is the situation with regard to marketing?

To be sure, progress has been made in product testing, evaluating consumer preferences, packaging, pricing, and so forth. The

* Marquis G. Eaton, *Financial Reporting in a Changing Society,* American Institute of Certified Public Accountants, New York, June 7, 1957.

large-scale development of "branded" products testifies to the validity of market analysis procedures. In addition, techniques of polling public opinion have improved considerably in recent years. But the failures—and indeed, the "whoppers"—that occur so often also testify to the uncertainties, to the large element of risk. We know really little about human motivation in relation to selling. We are just at the beginning of studies which lean on findings of the behavioral sciences.*

It is because of the imponderables and exaggerations that characterize advertising that we find merchandising a ripe field for satirical writing and, indeed, for a latter-day sort of muckraking. Every once in a while a book reaches the best seller list because of its "revelation," so to speak, of the "unseemly" aspects of advertising and selling. It is no wonder that marketing should seem thus to the outsider. For here we are dealing with the uncertainties of consumers' desires and tastes, with style and fashion, with a nation that has attained a luxury standard of living, whereas two generations ago much of our population was fortunate if it was able to maintain even a subsistence level of life. Under such circumstances, nonrational forces take over. And the more nonrational desires supplant rational ones, the more difficult does prediction become.

Indeed, in a world where the consumer is king, it is exceedingly difficult to establish any base stable enough for reliable prediction. The matter is just full of risks. The men who launched the Edsel can testify eloquently to this, and so can the executives who have weathered the ups and downs at Chrysler. "Two bad guesses," L. L. Colbert, President of the Chrysler Corporation, recently said to the Senate Antitrust and Monopoly Committee, "and we can easily be out of business." He testified how his company had guessed wrong in 1953 in assuming that consumers desired a simply styled car. At that time, he said, General Motors and Ford "went on the other way and we lost

* Joseph W. Newman, *Motivation Research and Marketing Management,* Harvard University Graduate School of Business Administration, Boston, 1957.

out." It was not only the large car but the extreme styling with upswept fins that enabled Chrysler to recapture its place in the industry by 1957.

Political Science

Of all the behavioral disciplines, political science should be expected to contribute most to the administrative phases of business activity. For essentially a corporation executive is entrusted with the government of a human institution. He is both lawmaker and law executor. He also dispenses justice and equity. He directs men individually and in groups. He exercises power over them.

But political science is an art and not a science. Even in its main area of study, the state, it has yielded few authoritative generalizations. Is the American constitutional system with its built-in checks and balances among executive, legislature, and judiciary the best type of government? Or is the British system superior, with its primary emphasis on executive responsibility? Is a bicameral legislature, such as our Congress, with chambers having equal power to be preferred? Or is the British model better, with the House of Commons having the power and the House of Lords serving largely in a ceremonial capacity? Are we clear about the comparative values of written and unwritten constitutions?

The debate over these and other questions is as old as history because they cannot be answered by measuring and counting, as is the practice in the laboratories of the natural sciences. The answer can come only out of human experience; we have to see how the tug of power among individuals and groups is accommodated and compromised. That is why practices vary so much among nations.

It is only utopians who achieve an ideal type of government, and their successes are confined largely to books, whether written by Plato, More, Butler, or Karl Marx. Mortal men have never been able to fulfill any of these dreams. And so political science, although yielding insights and perspective derived from the experience of government over the course of history with the problems of power, contributes little in the way of tools and skills that the business executive may utilize in carrying out his everyday responsibilities.

Statistics and Mathematics

The growing complexity of managerial decisions has in recent years stimulated interest and work in mathematics and statistical devices. Operations research and linear programing are among the developing tools that are already proving helpful in situations involving mass, quantitative data.

Undoubtedly there is a need for more rigorous and efficient methods of production scheduling, inventory control, and market forecasting. Accordingly, all of these statistical efforts are to be encouraged. As of the moment, however, they are empirical and in the experimental stage. To what extent they will supersede the sophisticated judgment of the experienced executive is difficult to predict. All one can say as of now and for some time to come is that these devices are likely to serve mainly as a check against, and help to, judgment. They cannot be said to constitute a tool upon which complete reliance may be placed.

15

Management and "Human Relations"

THE other social sciences—psychology, sociology, and anthropology—may best be considered under human relations, the term which has been given to the growing field of human behavior in industry. For, in truth, it is these three disciplines that make up the foundation underlying research and practice in human relations.

Interest in this subject was precipitated by the disintegrating forces of the Great Depression and the rise of the New Deal. Business was under severe attack as responsible for the breakdown in the American economic system. Legislation was enacted both to regulate various business activities and also to raise organized labor into a position of equality in bargaining power with corporations. Before long, massive militant organizing campaigns were launched to enroll union members in the heartland of American industry. Human relations arose, in a sense, as a countermove to this threat to corporations which had hitherto successfully resisted all attempts at unionization. Indeed it supplied business with an ideology—one of cooperation —as against the conflict let loose by unions with government encouragement.

The Harvard Business School became the center where the philosophy and content of the human relations school were developed. The then Dean, Wallace B. Donham, invited Elton Mayo to head the research of a group made up of anthropologists, sociologists, psychologists, and statisticians, in addition to men trained in business administration. The researchers were concentrated at the Hawthorne plant of the Western Electric Company. The reports constituted the first systematic exploration of human behavior in the work environment.

The concept of the social system, with its corollary of the informal social organization, was introduced from anthropology. Failure of communication in industry was identified as a major problem, among management personnel, between management and the rank and file at the workbench, and between those at the workbench and supervision.

The results of these researches and their implications were presented in published reports and meetings with representatives of management and institutions of learning. Relevant material was also gradually introduced into the curriculum of the Harvard Business School. Before long, other universities were undertaking research and teaching in human relations—sometimes independently but in most instances as part of newly established institutes of industrial relations, which had sprung up in many universities as an aftermath of the upheaval brought about by the massive militant organizing campaigns launched by new and old unions.

What has been the contribution of human relations? It must be said at once that because the work grew out of a specific, urgent need—industry at bay, so to speak, before a hostile government and an organized work force—much more was yielded in the form of insights and approaches to the problem of communication, supervisory training, and understanding of the executive function than was yielded by the traditional discipline of economics, upon which management had leaned as a guide to policy decisions.

Perhaps the greatest gain of all has been an enrichment of philosophy, a deeper understanding of human motivation, and an appreciation of the work environment as a human community. Morale has come to be seen as a complicated resultant of the interaction of the individual, already a complex psychological personality, and his group in workplace, home, and community. Thus, communication, admittedly a major unsolved problem, becomes more than simply telling people facts. They have to be listened to and understood before they can be made to understand, and often feelings and sentiments prove more potent as determinants of behavior than logic and reason. It follows that "listening" to people is as important as "telling" them, and at times much more so.

Again, role-playing—assuming the place of another in a given situation—was introduced as a helpful method of training supervisors to understand the people they led. Another contribution was greater awareness of the spontaneous growth of informal groups within office and shop as a means of resisting authority imposed from above.

All in all, the work in human relations has yielded a new dimension to executive training by orienting the administrator to the *totality* of his task in all its social as well as technical implications. But it has not given him precision tools for doing his task—or even for defining what the task should be. Failure to appreciate this is responsible for some of the dangerous overcommitments that some businessmen have been making.

Making People "Happy"

Some confusion has arisen about how far to go with the new insights provided by the social sciences. For example, does industry bear the responsibility to make its employees happy? Or to help them make a satisfactory adjustment to life and its problems? Could it do so, even if it so wished?

Obviously the well-managed company offers a propitious environment for the normal run of people to learn and master skills, as well as to experience social relationships that bring satisfaction. This is not to say, however, that industry can necessarily provide happiness or a cure for the anxieties and tensions characteristic of our times. Indeed, even with a sophisticated understanding of individual and social behavior, a supervisor in the shop or factory can do little directly for a maladjusted personality. His very position of authority limits his usefulness as a therapist.

Nor can a factory serve as a clinic or a place of treatment. It is a center where people are organized around a series of tasks to turn out products at a competitive cost. Next to the military, a factory is the most disciplined organization in modern society. Individuals and groups must fit into the organization. The justification for human relations is that it yields a better understanding of what can or cannot be done in the way of pushing limited personalities or recalcitrant groups toward the goals set by management. It does not equip management personnel with the training and experience necessary to handle personality problems or group maladjustments. Such problems had best be referred to community agencies staffed by social workers and psychotherapists.

We place an impossible burden upon management if we expect it to handle clinically the human problems within the work environment—prolific as they are. Indeed, one may well ask whether it might not be desirable to have at least one basic institution where life is disciplined. The nonjudgmental, all-accepting attitude has not resulted in those qualities of character essential in the rather harsh world of power which we have inherited even as late as the mid-twentieth century. Doubtless we need facilities for treating the sick and maladjusted, and in such specialized institutions a nonjudgmental approach is desirable. But are we as sure as we were a generation ago that such an atmosphere is desirable in all institutions, and particularly in the workplace?

The problem is sharpened by the implication that a sort of pledge is implicit in human relations to see to it that people are happy and satisfied. If the behavioral sciences which furnish the underpinnings of human relations are regarded as a way of gaining insight into human power and motivation, just as the physical sciences enable us to penetrate the secrets of natural power, to that extent the findings would be helpful in organizing work more effectively for production and making it more meaningful for those who produce. But once we assume the responsibility for human happiness, we put an impossible burden upon management.

Even if executives were willing to undertake such a responsibility, they would find themselves frustrated. They would be distracted from their main job of production. Moreover, even if they could acquire the expertness, they would find the treatment so long and protracted, the outcome so uncertain, that again frustration would result. On the other hand, the physician, the social worker, the psychiatrist undergo long training—both theoretical and clinical—specially directed to handle these problems. They are prepared for the difficulties to be encountered. The most expert in the field realize that, for those referred to them, human happiness may be an unattainable goal. They are content if, after treatment, tensions are alleviated and clients made more comfortable so that they can handle their problems without breakdowns.

16

Power and Amorality

THE limitations on management in carrying out the social and moral responsibilities to which many firms have become committed are even more serious and weighty than the limitations that arise in the philosophy of human relations. It is tempting for businessmen to overlook this fact. Having been under severe attack during the 1930s, and their legitimacy as custodians of economic life put on trial both here and abroad, they understandably have been reaching out for a moral rationale which would justify the wielding of great economic power under private auspices. Thus social and moral responsibility has become the theme of spokesmen for business.

Unrealistic Standards

Let it be said at once that a businessman is an inheritor of the Judaeo-Christian tradition, as well as of the equalitarian ethic of American democracy. As such he is always under the pressure of his conscience to apply the ideals of brotherhood, of fair dealing among men, of giving due consideration for the dignity and integrity of human personality.

In this sense all the debates as to whether religion and industry are contradictory or compatible are academic, if not meaningless. A businessman functions as a unitary personality, just as does any other man. He may formally practice religious worship only on the Sabbath when he goes to church. But he is the same man when he opens his office on Monday morning, always carrying his conscience with him as the overriding authority. For conscience constitutes the most potent as well as most pervasive system of power to which he is subject.*

At the same time, the management of a business is essentially a secular affair, subject to sin and error. Moreover, on the production floor, employees must fit into the organizational scheme. Goods must be turned out in quantity and quality as predetermined by management in its estimate of the market. The executive cannot treat everyone with strict equality; indeed, he must mete out rewards not only according to differences in ability, but according to his evaluation of ambition and potential for leadership. An employee may be less virtuous than another man, but if he excels in performance or future promise, he will be the likely one chosen for promotion.

In other words, the manager of an enterprise acts as a Christian but not as a Christian pastor, just as he acts as the head of a business but not as a father of a family. His office may be open to those who feel themselves aggrieved, but it cannot serve as a confessional, where everything is heard and forgiven. In fact, in the business office not everything that is heard may or can be forgiven. The needs and purpose of the business must always be kept in mind; if any man transgresses so much that production is imperiled, he must be warned, disciplined, and if no improvement is shown, eventually even discharged.

To hold up a standard of applying in any literal sense to workaday life the teaching of the Judaeo-Christian tradition is to put an impractical, if not impossible burden upon management. It is tantamount to no less than projecting the executive

* For an extended discussion of morality as power, see chap. 7, "The Power of Morality," in my book, *Power and Morality in a Business Society*, McGraw-Hill Book Company, Inc., New York, 1956.

group into a situation of perpetual sinfulness. Indeed, an executive may, under these circumstances, develop a pervasive sense of guilt. He may become immobilized for practical action, incapable of giving his best to the community.

One has only to ponder the difficulties implicit in applying Judaeo-Christian ethics to many phases of business activity to realize what a heavy, if not impossible, burden such an attempt would put upon management. Hardly a day passes but what an executive faces decisions that are freighted with ethical ambiguity. He may have to replace existing equipment by more automatic machinery, enlarge or shut down plants, move from old to new centers, and so on. Any or all of these decisions, although beneficial in the long run, carry immediate privation or injury to people, to towns, to ways of life.

The Revolutionists

Indeed, to put it bluntly, the businessman is a destroyer even as he builds. He is the major revolutionist of our times; he is always searching for new products, new materials, new resources, new machines, new skills, new markets, constantly changing styles and fashions. He encourages and practices obsolescence. In the end, the community as a whole may be wealthier for all this, but in the transition much is wasted that is still useful. This is disturbing, as we all know, to many men concerned with moral values, for they see economic waste as a symptom of an overly materialistic emphasis.

Even more serious from the moralist's viewpoint is the fact that a varying number of human beings may be expendable. Will old employees prove as adaptable as newly hired, younger men to machinery bought to decrease costs and strengthen the company's competitive position? Is the union with which the company deals justified in demanding wage increases, fringe benefits, and other improvements? If not, should the executive face the possibility of a strike, which means a resort to power?

And what about the delicate ethical questions that are cast up by a strike? For instance, how should management treat strikers when they return? And if during their absence, some of their jobs were taken over by those who continued to work, or even by new employees, who should be moved or displaced?

Or take the situation when management faces the decision as to whether or not to move a factory from a Northern to a Southern town. Economic factors and profitability are major criteria. But the plant may be the main industry of the town. The townsfolk are certain to suffer injury. Jobs will be destroyed. Privation will be imposed upon workers, merchants, grocers, landlords. What is the executive to do?

On technical grounds, he decides that he cannot equalize costs between where he is and where he may go. He had, therefore, better move. But technical considerations are largely matters of judgment; they are not precise criteria like those available to a scientist in a laboratory. And so conscience will doubtless trouble the man who makes the final decision. He will spend many a sleepless night pondering the right course of action. In the end, however, he is most likely to decide on moving; when the "chips are down," prudence in terms of cost determines final action.

Of course, he will try to diminish the damage he is doing to his old townsfolk as much as possible by paying separation wages, offering to help some to move, encouraging industry to move into the town, and so on. Nevertheless, the damage will be considerable. This country is full of ghost towns created by the migration of industry. Yet the men who made these decisions were morally sensitive men, conditioned to all the values of their Judaeo-Christian heritage.

Technical "Musts"

The truth of the matter is that business as business and industry as industry operate in an amoral, technical world.

A policy decision is a form of power, and it is amoral as is all power. Consequently every businessman is constantly carrying on a dialogue on the theme; "the technical *must* versus the ethical *ought*." * Conscience does act as a check, but essentially a great many decisions must be based on technical considerations—on productivity, costs, proximity to markets, competitive conditions. No businessman dares for long to be too far ahead of his competition in the performance of social and moral responsibilities. His main concern is survival.

The environment in which business operates sets limits to the scope of action of any individual executive. I am not, of course, talking about elementary things like honesty, kindness, charity, or observation of the requirements of the law, but rather about broad economic factors. For example, it has been the constant complaint of industrialists in New England that they suffer adversely in competition with the South; social legislation and strong labor unions result in higher wages, larger social security benefits, more costly conditions of work, and so on. If such a condition continues indefinitely, the most moral businessman must shut up shop ultimately and move to states with lower costs—if he is to survive in a competitive world.

The point I am trying to make is that all this is not a matter of virtue or evil. The heart of business consists of a technical activity to produce goods and services at a price which will enable management to stay in business, recoup its costs, allow for depreciation, make it possible to attract capital, and be in the vanguard of advancing technology. It is only as management becomes involved with other people—with labor, with consumers, with competitors—that moral issues arise.

If the tensions of conscience were not constantly at play, the forces of competition would tend to degrade standards to the lowest common denominator. But, man being only man, conscience frequently yields to prudence. Hence—and this is vitally important—it is in the interest of the community that manage-

* For fuller discussion of this question see chap. 5, "The Power of Business," *ibid.*

ment be checked by the power of unions and government. For conscience needs an ally in the form of costs—possible losses through strikes or government regulation to serve as a counter-weight to the costs based on the self-interest of profitability. Without counter-power, the necessity to be practical as a way of ensuring survival in a competitive world would win out in the debate of the "ethical *ought* versus the technical *must.*"

We should bear in mind, moreover, that the pressure by unions and government tends to equalize labor and other social costs among competitors. In the long run, therefore, these costs become absorbable just like the cost of machinery and materials. Thus, power which is amoral in itself helps to make morality attainable.

In the meanwhile, though we fail in the day-to-day application of Judaeo-Christian virtues, the very act of aspiration keeps the battle for moral values alive. His own conscience is every executive's battlefield for ethical goals, to be reached as, and when, they become practically attainable. (It is because of the necessity to make critical decisions under conditions of technical uncertainty and moral ambiguity, by the way, that the case method has emerged as the most effective tool for business education.)

It is this gap between the practical and the ideal, and not the gap between good and evil, that explains the belated acceptance of economic and social measures such as social insurance, vacations and holidays with pay, shorter hours of work, call-in pay, separation wages, standards of pay that will yield more than a subsistence wage, and so on. As the twentieth century advanced it was only as enough pressure was put upon all business by trade unions or by government—or both—that standards of human relations were raised. Since the additional costs entailed became gradually uniform for all enterprises in a given industry, competition reached a higher level. The morally sensitive person could then operate his business with a better conscience.

Wrong Promises?

The underlying difficulty in achieving, in the here and now, the fulfillment of moral aspirations by individual business enterprises has been obscured by the boom prosperity under which we have been living in recent years. Significantly, it is a prosperity attributable *not* so much to private enterprise as to a number of unusual factors, such as the abnormal demands of war since the early 1940s, pent-up consumer demands after the war, the need to shore up and rearm the free world, the large budget required by our defense posture, and the commitment to full employment as a goal of the entire community and the resultant mild inflation. All of these things have made for a feeling of well-being; the harshness of criticism of the New Deal days has diminished considerably.

But this is the first time that we have experienced so long a period of good times. We have only to look back to the prosperity of the 1920s and the collapse of the 1930s to realize how foolhardy it is to give the impression that private enterprise and business management are responsible either for prosperity or depression. We are far from having learned as yet the way to solve the basic problems of modern industrial society. We may well be on the road to mitigating the harsh impact of unemployment and social maladjustment, but to give the impression that we have mastered the complex problems of seasonal, cyclical, and secular fluctuations, of shifting markets, is surely utopian.

If business management is thought capable of guaranteeing the same kind of prosperity as has characterized the past fifteen years, the community is surely in for disappointment and disillusionment. The greater the commitment to social responsibility, the greater the likelihood that business will be blamed just as it was in the 1930s. It is well to recall how business was "declassed" when the crash came in 1929, becoming the scapegoat and the object of hostility for the privation suffered by unemployed workers, dispossessed farmers, and embittered intellectuals.

Onus Is on the Public

Indeed, until we master the complexities underlying the causes of instability it is hardly fair to attribute major responsibility to management. Instability is the responsibility of all of us. It is a price we pay for decentralization of economic power, for assuring maximum freedom to manager, worker, and consumer. Consequently it is the job of all of us working through government to wrestle with the problems of declining industries and regions, of the impact of new technologies, of recession and depression, as well as of inflation during prosperity. No one business or group of businesses alone can muster the resources to prevent these abnormal events from occurring or alleviate the human consequences when they do occur.

As a case in point, take the mild but gradual inflation that we have experienced in the past decade. The dollar is shrinking in value year by year. We all talk about it. Businessmen and labor are admonished to exercise self-restraint so as not to put upward pressure upon prices.

But all this talk, whether by Roosevelt, Truman, or Eisenhower, has proved utterly unavailing. Prices continue their upward course, money its downward course. It is not because labor or businessmen are evil or unpatriotic that stable prices are not realized. It is because the social and economic factors are too complex and beyond the reach of any particular business or individual. Management does not find it possible to stabilize prices no matter how much it wishes to arrest the inflationary spiral. Nor can labor leaders resist the pressure from their ranks for higher wages and other benefits. If inflation can be stopped at all, the means seems to be an appropriate fiscal and monetary policy.

Obviously, in the case of problems like depression, inflation, or full employment, it is not private business but government acting for the entire community that must assume responsibility and take appropriate action. Under such circumstances, is it not foolhardy, if not dangerous, for management to make moral commitments which are beyond its ability to fulfill? Is it fair to management and, indeed, to the community to set up standards of performance and expectations beyond the state of knowledge, technical skill, and available tools? Is it wise to make lofty moral and ethical commitments when any day ideals may have to give way to the grim necessity of cutting costs so sharply that human beings inevitably suffer?

To continue to do so is only to "come a cropper" when the day of reckoning comes. Those of us who have lived through the prosperity of the 1920s, when businessmen were heroes, and the Depression of the 1930s, when overnight the same men became villains, do not wish to see such an episode repeated. The stakes are too great not only for the solvency and vitality of our domestic life, but also for the maintenance of our leadership of the free world as we seek to stem the tide of Communist imperialism.

17

Difficulty of Sanctions

ANOTHER consideration is involved in this discussion of moral responsibilities. One should not overlook the fact that it is exceedingly difficult, if not almost impossible, for the business community itself to enforce ethical and moral standards. Indeed, there is no way by means of which to formulate an ethical code of universal acceptance. For business is not yet a profession in the complete sense of the word; nor is it, as indicated previously, a movement like the AFL-CIO.

In well-developed professions, such as medicine or law, ethical codes are formulated and enforced; the penalty is expulsion. Moreover, entrance into the profession is by examination. The examination leads to a licensing procedure. Thus, violation of the ethical codes means not only expulsion for the wrongdoer, but inability to continue in practice.

Such procedures are not open to business. Anyone can enter into business; anyone can start his own firm. Expulsion from a trade organization is no serious penalty; it is known only to the insiders, and it has little effect on the consumers whom the business serves.

Sense of Identity Important

Because labor and trade unionism constitute a movement, expulsion from the central federation discredits the union or the leadership. But even so, the AFL was very slow and reluctant to formulate ethical codes and to enforce them. Neither Samuel Gompers nor William Green would take any action that would place the central federation in a position of responsibility for corrupt and questionable practices on the parts of leaders of individual unions. They always took the position that these unions were autonomous and that the questions had to be raised within themselves. To the extent that law was violated, they felt it was up to public authorities through the enforcement of civil and criminal law to bring the guilty parties to the bar.

With the succession of George Meany as President of the AFL, a different line was established. Meany took the position that corruption in any union affiliated with the AFL *was* the business of the federation. And one of the early acts of his administration was to expel the International Longshoremen's Association, when corrupt practices came to light. With the joining of the CIO and the AFL into one labor movement, codes of fair practices became the first order of business. They were formulated and they have been enforced. Unlike business corporations, individual unions feel deeply the stigma of expulsion. Even as strong a union as the teamsters is anxious to be reinstated within the house of labor.

It is the feeling of identity with labor, and the desire to have mutual bonds with all unions, that makes every union prize highly its affiliation with a strong labor movement. The same cannot be said for members of the National Association of Manufacturers, the United States Chamber of Commerce, and various trade associations. Membership is no matter of great importance. The United States Steel Corporation, for instance, can get along very well without belonging to any association.

Thus any attempt by an industry or trade association to formulate ethical codes, although perhaps desirable as a matter of setting standards which members would like to see observed, could not result in the same degree of sanction as is true of organized labor. Expulsion would mean very little in the way of penalty.

Avoiding Embarrassment

The point I am making is that the difficulty of invoking sanctions is another reason for being cautious when speaking for business. We do not want to give the impression that ethical practices are enforceable. There are good reasons for this. Every once in a while, the public is shocked by revelations of questionable, if not corrupt, practices on the part of certain businessmen. Be it direct cash, or gifts in the form of minks or vicuna, deep freezes or expensive rugs, or the general practice of lavish entertainment at businessmen's expense—all these things shock the community and shake the confidence of the everyday citizen in the integrity of business as well as of those in government service.

It is exceedingly embarrassing to find a Cabinet officer seeking to direct government business to a company in which he has an interest. It is even more embarrassing to have people who are in the White House and at the right hand of the President take gifts from businessmen and later on intercede for them. Yet in this imperfect world, such things happen from time to time. Accordingly, it is best to be cautious, to make limited commitments, and to be sure that those made are carried out.

Undoubtedly, the business community, and those who are interested in the development of a professional attitude and ethical standards, must give serious thought as to how to formulate an acceptable moral code and enforce it. But the difficulties are great. For, as long as entry to business is free, as it must be in a democratic society, and as long as no one has to obtain a license to practice industrial management, it will be difficult to develop and enforce codes of ethical practices.

The real problem is how to develop codes and philosophies which will become so acceptable as a matter of *custom* that the individual who is guilty of violating them more or less becomes an outcast. To this end, perhaps there should be standing committees in the various trades that would publicly condemn those businesses and corporations guilty of questionable practices, just as the AFL-CIO has done publicly in the case of trade unions found guilty of corrupt practices.

18

Adding to the Illusion

I HAVE mentioned several ways in which business leaders have created—often unwittingly—an illusion of omnipotence. There is still another way that needs to be considered. It is, in fact, so symptomatic of the general problem we are discussing, and poses such an important issue, that I shall single it out for special attention.

I refer to the prevailing standards of executive compensation. Given the technical limitations of management under the present state of the art of administration, can the high emoluments paid to corporate executives be justified? Whether the president of a corporation is entitled, by virtue of profits, total sales, or some other test, to the compensation agreed upon between him and the board of directors is not the question. If the man who is responsible for the creation of wealth for stockholders is worthy of substantial payment in their eyes, if the matter could be considered a private, domestic one within the four walls of the corporation, then any salary might be justified.

But business now operates in a goldfish bowl and, in reality, takes on more and more the characteristics of a public trust. The larger the corporation, the more is this the case. Moreover, because of the moral affirmations which businessmen have been articulating in recent years and because of the pledge to direct business activities toward ethical goals, materialistic standards alone can no longer be applied. If they are, and if businessmen exact remuneration completely out of all scale with that paid other groups concerned with the public good, management is in a perilous condition of being suspect.

Vulnerability to Attack

Those who attack business in political and labor circles find ready ammunition in the high compensation paid corporate executives. The facts are made public in labor journals —and in a sarcastic manner—as exemplified by the comments in the monthly publication of the AFL-CIO for June, 1957: *

> There must be something radically wrong with "incentive" bonus systems for executives in quite a few companies. Many companies also must be running into trouble, trying to keep down "inflationary" salary increases for their top officers.
>
> Bethlehem Steel, for example, paid its chairman Eugene G. Grace, $150,000. in base pay last year. His bonuses, however, came to $659,011 —more than four times his base pay. The total was $809,011. in 1956— a 14.6% salary increase above the $705,923. paid to Mr. Grace in 1955. Didn't we hear some rumor that such a $103,000. wage increase—or even a $100 increase—is inflationary?
>
> U.S. Steel, which strongly holds the line against "inflation" by raising steel prices twice a year, paid its chairman Roger Blough, $264,900. in 1956. That was a 19.2% increase above his 1955 salary.
>
> We wonder who negotiates these boosts for executive big shots?

The issue with regard to high compensation comes dramatically to the fore when a prominent corporation president is appointed to high office, such as a Cabinet post. In confirmation hearings before Senate committees the appointee seems to be in a morally indefensible position. It is not only the large annual salary that

* "Who Negotiates For These Execs?" *Economic Trends and Outlook,* AFL-CIO Economic Policy Committee, vol. 2, no. 6, June, 1957.

raises eyebrows but even more the stockholdings and other emoluments which go to make up executive compensation. The erstwhile executive squirms when he realizes that he will have to divest himself of such holdings at perhaps a substantial loss. And how about the pensions and consulting fees he is to receive from his corporation when he retires? Thus what was perfectly acceptable practice within the corporate framework now runs into a possible "conflict of interest," if not an implicit moral offense.

Even more serious, compensation of the dimensions now in practice conveys the image of supermen. A man worth 200,000 dollars a year or more must, in the eyes of the man in the street, be a genius who has it in his power to control economic factors so as to avoid recessions, unemployment, and so forth. Accordingly, when things do not go right, when men have to be laid off or put on part time, or told that the wage they ask is too high, they simply disbelieve what they hear or become cynical.

The rich man has always been "on trial" from Biblical days on. The owner-executive of the nineteenth and early twentieth century had difficulties enough in winning acceptance of the legitimacy of his wealth. But at least he was the owner. The majority of contemporary corporation presidents have no such title to large incomes. The moral framework is different. The owner made sacrifices, took risks. Together with his family and friends he developed a business. Later they may all have become partners, or if incorporated, holders of the stock. By contrast, the modern executive may hold little or no stock in the business he manages. He may come into it long after it is already a going concern. Yet he may receive compensation running into six figures.

But if a man has the ability to handle the complexities of a modern corporation, why should he not be paid a high salary, whether he owns property or not? Indeed, should the act not be applauded as an expression of the American creed that ability rather than property should be rewarded? The answer is yes—*provided* the salary does not offend some other equally fundamental sentiment.

I suspect that the heart of the matter lies in the fact that compensation of corporate executives is way out of line with standards already established for positions enjoying the very highest moral and social prestige. Is it the part of wisdom to pay the president of a corporation a larger salary than the nation pays the President of the United States? Should anyone receive more than the man who occupies the most exalted position, has the greatest honor the nation can bestow, and carries the heaviest burden of responsibility perhaps of any man in the world? The same question might be raised relative to the salaries of the Supreme Court justices and Cabinet members.

Since it can hardly be said that business leaders' responsibilities are greater, or that their positions are more exalted than those of the highest public officers, it would seem that they exact so large a toll because of the strategic role they play in the materialistic world of wealth, that we as a nation reward the man who makes money much more liberally than the man who leads the nation in the White House, or presides over the highest court of the land, or is put at the head of the armed forces in time of war.

Fresh Look Needed

The size of the compensation typically paid corporation presidents leads to expectancies of performance which under conditions of uncertainty cannot be delivered, especially during years of crises. It is then that emotions are aroused. Those suffering privations look for a scapegoat. The rich—or those thought to be rich—are the natural victims for such a role. Thus in times of hardship, latent hostility toward what is deemed an inequitable distribution of wealth becomes a threat to the unity of the nation. Punitive legislation frequently results, as, for example, confiscatory taxation which at certain levels "expropriates" 90 per cent of earnings.

But then a vicious circle is set in motion: payments for business executives are put at even higher figures; instead of direct pay, corporations devise various substitutes which may escape the ax of the tax collector in any given year. Thus, morality is further tarnished by "duplicity" of lush expense accounts, consultantships after retirement, deferred annuities, life insurance for dependents, stock options under favorable circumstances, and so on.

Has not the time come for a fresh, heart-searching evaluation of our scale of values in determining compensation for significant services in our society, especially in view of the moral posture businessmen have been assuming in recent years?

The Businessman's Business

Precisely because of the strategic role played by members of the managerial group in our society as custodians of our economic institutions, it is important to keep in mind the limitations under which they work—limitations of tools, of science, of predicting accurately basic economic and social factors. Yet the businessman must make decisions of grave consequence every day of his life, entailing a considerable risk and margin of error. He should, therefore, try to avoid giving the impression of a sort of perfectionism by the moral commitments he makes as spokesman for private enterprise. For with such commitments goes the danger of being blamed as a failure and scapegoat for the instability that characterizes our kind of free society.

Would it not serve the public interest best to restore the businessman to his traditional role as a creator of wealth, to respect him as such, to pay him (but not overpay him) what he is worth in terms of service to the community, and to encourage him to go forward with the greatest possible speed in the job we entrust to him—the creation of as strong a material foundation as possible for our society? Surely the human and social problems that are concomitant with creativity in industry must be dealt with, but let us not make management the agency of primary responsibility. Other institutions—public and private—can undertake this task much more effectively.

PART V

Wanted: a Technical Framework

19

An Economics for Business Administrators

IF businessmen are to be in a position to discharge their obligations to the corporations which they manage, and at the same time further moral goals, they must have available, to begin with, a technical framework so that they may make intelligent and effective decisions both in planning and in execution. The core of the technical framework must consist of what are generally termed economic factors: capital must be raised, plants built, machinery obtained, raw materials bought, labor engaged and trained to carry forward the necessary operations. The goods and services must be priced and sold. These constitute essentially the activities with which economics deals.

But these economic activities are carried on within a community involving men and women in various capacities—as employees, as customers, as bankers, as suppliers, and as citizens who make up public opinion and, indeed, are responsible for laws affecting industry. Any corporation, moreover, is in itself a social institution, in which both cooperation and conflict are present—between supervisors and employees, between management and unions, between the company and its competitors, and between it and various government agencies.

The technical framework, therefore, although having as its core concepts from economics, must also integrate elements from psychology, sociology, anthropology, and political science. In brief, it should be a combination of economics and human relations. In addition, of course, management must be aware of technological developments: new machinery, new methods, new materials, and better ways of handling old problems. Modern social and economic life has been projected on advancing technology. Finally, since every business operates in the moral climate of our Judaeo-Christian tradition, management must give heed to moral and ethical tenets. Indeed economics, human relations, technology, and moral values are interrelated and make up an organic whole as a business gets going and functions from day to day.

In the next few chapters, we shall devote ourselves to the consideration of a technical framework and leave for following chapters a similar exploration of an appropriate moral framework. Both are interdependent. We cannot achieve moral goals unless a business is managed successfully, that is to say, unless it survives. Survival and morality must go hand in hand. Under certain emergencies like war or persecution, one is willing to perish for treasured beliefs in order to conserve moral goals. But these are not the situations we are discussing in this book; rather, we are examining the conduct of normal social and economic life.

Need for a New Economics

Few are the practical men, the administrators in business, government, unions, or any area of economic responsibility, who have not in recent years craved a workable economics to guide policy and action. The perplexed, of course, constitute an enduring variety of Homo sapiens. But in our ominous times and foreboding world, perplexity has become so generic a feature of life that even those on whom we are accustomed to depend for guidance seem themselves perplexed, while their conflicting counsels add to the mounting confusion.

Events crowd in so rapidly that yesterday's programs lose relevance for today's problems. We already are discovering that policies framed to lift depression and avert underconsumption do not fit the needs of full employment and prosperity. We have seen the long-run fears of stagnation in a "mature economy" give way to the precisely polarized alarms of inflation in a capacity-producing economy.

Space, as well as time—or shall we say geography, as well as history—subjects economic theory to new and sharp tests of concrete practice. Schools of economic doctrine no longer confine their clashes to the libraries or the classrooms or the soapboxes. Critical economic issues impinge upon every man's everyday living, everywhere. Thus enterprise economics, socialist economics, communist economics, all continuously changing as their proponents continue to argue about what is and what ought to be, now have graduated from exclusively theoretical debates into rivalries of contemporaneous social systems. Now they all can—and should—be judged by their works.

If we in the United States have at times in very recent years yielded to excessive pessimism, to oversensitivity about our failures, we can by that very token look again at the whole record. There is good reason why, in economic as in foreign affairs, our self-searching has never yet undermined our fundamental strengths. If again a renewed note of faith and confidence appears in our self-scrutiny, there are questions still to be answered in the affirmations as well as in the criticisms. For instance: is it simply a combination of historical accidents that explains why we find ourselves, in spite of all our unsolved problems, enjoying (compared with any other nation) the highest wages, the best working conditions, the highest profits, the highest standard of living—and, at the same time, the highest degree of liberty?

Granting all our favoring circumstances, granting all the lacks upon which we still have to improve, what have we done over the years and what are we doing day in and day out to have already brought to fruition so unique an achievement?

By the very measures of our recorded accomplishments, our current strengths, and our future expectancies, is it not incumbent upon us to try to discover the dynamic elements, the cohesive forces that keep going this intricate mechanism we know as our American industrial society?

John Commons's Contribution

In my opinion, an appropriate economics for our purpose can be found in the works of John R. Commons. His three major books, *The Economics of Collective Action,** *Legal Foundations of Capitalism,*† and *Institutional Economics: Its Place in Political Economy,*‡ embody the mature thinking and experience of a pioneering American economist.

Essentially Commons deals with industry as a going human institution in which decisions are constantly made and based upon the interaction of individuals and groups. In other words, to him a business is a *social* institution whose primary purpose is economic; its job is to make available goods and services to the community. It is for that reason that the school of economics which he helped found and of which he was a prime leader is sometimes called institutional economics.

Unfortunately, under the impact of latter-day mathematical and "model" economics, this school is out of fashion now. Although the school itself may not be revived by professional economists, it is significant that the impact of the behavioral sciences and human relations on industry and management is

* Edited by Kenneth H. Parson, with a biographical sketch by Selig Perlman, The Macmillan Company, New York, 1950.

† The Macmillan Company, New York, 1924.

‡ The Macmillan Company, New York, 1934.

virtually introducing a new type of institutional economics. To be sure, it is not called that, but if the reader will follow me in the analysis about to be made, I think he will see for himself its relevance for present-day management as operators of a modern corporation in its technical, economic, and human setting.

When Commons began the formulation of his theoretical system in the 1920s, he was already recognized as the outstanding historian and analyst of labor in the United States. But his concrete experience ramified into many other sectors of economic activity, and significantly, he drew his first basic concepts for systemizing that experience from the study of court decisions. His critical evaluation of traditional economic theory aligned him with the characteristically Anglo-American "institutionalists" like Thorstein Veblen in the United States and R. H. Tawney in Britain. But, as we shall see, he differed from them in evaluating business as an American institution.

The very nature of Commons's work—every major strand of it—gives his economics immediate relevance and timeliness. For he makes organized activity the very foundation of economics and group association the instrument of such economic action. He starts with the three group organizations—corporation, union, and government—that are at the very heart of our present-day problem. They give more than a starting point, however; they underwrite the approach to all economic exploration upon which Commons insists and which he himself consistently follows. Only an economics of *collective,* as distinguished from individual, action can prove fruitful, he maintains, for understanding what is going on around us. But it is always *action* that concerns him; the words are continuously combined —in titles as in text—and even so he does not find normal phrasing completely satisfactory to establish this linkage of structure and activity. He seeks to evoke the sense of volitional social process by recourse to the hyphen: in his economics he studies man's will-in-action, traces human pursuit of individual purposes in society through collectives-in-action, projects the state as politicians-in-action, the corporation as businessmen-in-action, and the union as unionists-in-action.

Directing his thinking toward such questions, Commons constructed a system of economics that explores the mechanisms by which a going society resolves successive problems as they arise, rather than one that offers set solutions for economic problems themselves. Thus his work proves itself a major contribution toward illuminating the nature of the administrative process as a decision-making activity.

Group Organization

Let us consider, first, the element in that process upon which Commons grounds all else: the *structure* of economic action constituted by the network of group associations which make our society.

In the light of recent events it may, at first, appear that Commons chose an unfortunate term for these omnipresent associations when he called them "collectives." To our contemporary ears, the word immediately suggests "collectivism"—the supremacy of one major collective, the political party, in a government-dominated society. Actually, Commons rejected every variant of encroaching "totalitarianism." He wrote at a time when quasi-surrender to "inevitable social trends" was still strong; confidence had not yet been recaptured in human controls over economic forces; yet he was convinced that we in this country could continue to build a free, progressive society, if we so willed and acted with courage.

His confidence was buttressed not only by the record of objective accomplishment but also by his estimate of the practical idealism, the technical proficiency, and the buoyant democracy of the American people. His admiration for his countrymen encompassed all ranks. He recalled with relish the titans he had personally known, from Andrew Carnegie to Samuel Gompers, from Frederick Taylor to Robert La Follette, as well as the individual printers, steel men, railroaders, and tailors beside whom he had worked in his early years or whom he later had studied at their work.

Salty, resourceful American individualists though these people were, he noted that they behaved in their economic roles as *corporation* executives, *shop* supervisors, *union* leaders, *union* members, and *shop* employees. Even upon the Anglo-American soil of traditional individualism, to put it shortly, man acts by and with groups. When the group assumes formal organization, it acquires leaders, ranks, and jointly formulated rules. Thereby the institution appears—whether it be the corporation, the union, or the state.

Though the institution is thus a natural growth, collectivism as such is by no means inevitable. We have our choices, our alternatives; we are never merely passive driftwood on the currents of historic tendency, or even fated instruments of social destiny. But it is well to remember that these choices too lie within the decisions of organized groups, not autonomous individuals.

The Passing of "Economic Man"

Today this concept of the group beyond the individual as the prime agent in social action hardly seems to need the elaborate evidence Commons marshaled to establish it. Indeed, even when he began more than a quarter-century ago to build his own system of institutional economics, the concept of "economic man" was already under sharp attack. But, in Commons's view, even the multiplying revisions of "economic man" did not project an economics adequate for the recognizable practical world of modern industrialism. Economic theory requires more than the replacement of a "rational pecuniary man" by a nonrational folk man, or by an instinctive Freudian man, or by a reflex-conditioned physiologic man, or by any other kind of modified but still central individual. A realistic theory requires that individual man be seen as a member of organized groups of men. For these organized groups power the economy and thus constitute the proper and the prime study of economics.

Commons liked to recall how persistently throughout our history practice and theory had diverged in this sector of analysis. Even while the classical economists were placing the individual at the source of all economic action, the individuals themselves, as everyday economic practitioners, were fighting for the right to act in combination.

The protracted struggle of labor to establish its right to organize is the most recent chapter in this experience. It is still so vivid in our minds that we are inclined to forget that the corporation, too, represents a parallel right of association which businessmen, in their earlier turn, had similarly won only by hard and purposeful campaigning. The right to incorporate, precisely like the right to unionize, expanded and liberated individual action, even as it also controlled its constituent individuals; each right generated an industrial institution. If we accept the general incorporation statute enacted by Connecticut and New Hampshire in 1837 as the prototype of modern limited liability law,* business thus established its right to act collectively for economic purposes precisely one century before the National Labor Relations Act was validated by the Supreme Court.

By still another parallel development, the political party in its modern form has also emerged from progressive battles for group recognition and new freedoms. The right to vote and hold government position became universal only as successive groups won removal of the bars against them (qualification of property,

* Commons, *The Economics of Collective Action*, pp. 314–317. Cf. also E. Merrick Dodd, "The Evolution of Limited Liability in American Industry: Massachusetts," *Harvard Law Review*, vol. 61, no. 8, pp. 1351–1379, September, 1948. The process of validation by state law was not completed until the 1880s. Then the struggle entered its next stage when business corporations sought the right to combine.

religion, race, or sex). Even then, for all the counting of the *individual* ballots, political action soon became collective also. Political parties, unnoted and unprovided for by the founders of our nation, proved before long to be the true instruments of government through majority party administration, minority party opposition, and continuing party machines.

Here then is a salutary datum to hold clearly in the forefront of present-day thinking: this reminder that all three of the "big" organizations dominating our industrial society, the business corporation and the democratic state quite as much as the labor union, represent rights of associated action first hard won and then progressively developed by free men over long decades of individual effort and experience.

Inadequacy of Early Theories

To be sure, Adam Smith and those who followed him were also seeking to "free" men by securing for them new rights of action. They were attempting to cut from the pioneering activities of businessmen who were effectuating the Industrial Revolution the hampering interferences interposed by the associations and institutions surviving from the predecessor mercantilist society. But they failed to realize that, eventually, effective adaptations would have to be from one network of group organizations to another. Instead, they made economic action on every sector of the new society an arithmetic exercise in addition—the sum of individual actions which operated, under favoring conditions for pursuing self-interest responsibly, to yield the general good.

No doubt, economists have always been influenced by the sciences of their day that were capturing the imagination of men. Commons traced the central intellectual interrelations through multiple schools of doctrine, somewhat as follows:

At the close of the eighteenth century, Newtonian mechanics furnished the model for Adam Smith and his followers as they sought freedom for the new enterprisers from the restrictions of the old guilds, the monopoly companies, and the regulatory state. The move to place at the core of economics an atomistic individual who promised to increase the wealth of nations if left free to advance his own proper ends was thus buttressed by intellectual respectability. Much as the solar system and each of its units in the physical universe moved within calculable orbits under the pull of gravitational forces, so society and each of its constituent individuals moved within orbits of automatic progress under the pull of enlightened self-interest.

During the second half of the nineteenth century when capitalism was expanding, Darwinian biology supplemented Newtonian physics. Economic man emerged as the strong individual in the inescapable struggle for existence. Society, like nature, became a harsh but still beneficently progressive organism of selective adaptation by which the fit survived to advance evolutionary improvement.

Later, mathematics, psychology, and other sciences exerted their influence, although not projecting quite so pervasive a mold for economic thought as a whole as did the sciences of Newton and Darwin. Also, economic theories were modified to mesh better with changing economic practices in our society. For example, certain schools, though retaining some particular variant of rational economic man at the core of social action, sought to recast the concepts of individual motivation in terms of markets and the "price system." Others began to trace the drives toward group organization.

In the studies of group organization, Commons saw the larger and more enduring significance. For all their promising and often illuminating insights, however, these schools of "societal" economics (if a comprehensive label for them may be coined) proved finally inadequate for explaining the highly complex and pluralistic nature of modern industrialism, particularly in its Western democratic frame of development. Some of their protagonists scrutinized piecemeal one form of advancing group organization after another, without charting the actual evolution of the economy as a whole. Some did attempt a more rounded exploration of "pecuniary" civilization, but seemed to be studying present realities only for purposes of deprecatory contrast with an idealized past or an idealized future. Whatever in the total concrete actuality ran counter to their preconceived models they passed over.

Thus they disregarded the violence and exclusiveness of the preindustrial communities toward outsiders and saw only their qualities of mutual concern toward those within their own small circles. By the same token, they overlooked, when portraying the capitalist spirit, its advancing, proliferating ethical attitudes, such as the prestige values accorded to conscientious payment of debts, to good-will services and fair value to customers, to increasing responsibility for workers, to the trusteeship concept of wealth. They concentrated instead so strongly upon "unlimited pecuniary self-seeking," which furnished presumably the exclusive energizer of business, that Western democracy finally became for them "the acquisitive society."

The inadequacy of such systems in Commons's eyes was not just a matter of the intangible features of an economy—its ethos or rationale—but also concerned its human types. He might share—as he did—Thorstein Veblen's admiration for the technician, but these production specialists comprised for him simply one order of industrial leadership. He explicitly refused to follow Veblen in idealizing engineers, who turned out tangible goods, for the purposes of contrast with businessmen, who juggled the intangible "make-believe" of the price system to "get something for nothing."

Instead Commons saw each type of industrial leader playing its respectively important role in the whole economy. If engineers contributed toward technical functioning, and so toward man's relations to nature via the application of physical science, corporation executives contributed to the social functioning of the economy, to "man's relations to other men." There were always and everywhere three interdependent but distinct components in our economics—human organism, technical mechanism, and social organization.

"Going Concern"

All lines of analysis thus led Commons back to his first principles:

1. The labor union, the political state, and equally business management must be specifically understood as group organizations, collectives, conditioning human activities in our present-day American economy.

2. They are all in their origins tools of man's needs and purposes in industrial society, in varying ways running now along parallel courses, again crashing in head-on conflict, finally forging a length of common, or at least intermeshing, trails.

3. The dynamism of the group organizations constitutes an integral feature of their characteristic structure; they are indeed essentially men interacting, representing always, by the tests of Commons's foundational definition, "collective action in liberation, expansion, and control of individual action."

No wonder the term "going concern" seemed to Commons an apt descriptive label not only for the business corporation but also for all institutions. But though he borrowed this term from the courts, he did not accept the limitations of "artificiality" there included in it. The judges, from Chief Justice Marshall on, had under this title progressively defined the rights and duties of the business corporation as those of an "artificial person created by law." For Commons, the organized groups—all of them "going concerns"—which regulated human activity existed prior to any formal legal establishment. They were as fundamental, indeed, as man's impulse to act with his fellows.

Of course, formal organization usually followed in time. But the act of conscious organization—the charter, compact, or constitution that transformed individuals into corporations, unions, or political entities—still did not create a "going concern." Nor did the formalization reduce any one of them to "a mere sum total of individuals, on the one hand, (or to) an abstract entity, on the other." Instead, each going concern developed over a period of time its own "working rules . . . operating through the actions and transactions of those who observe the rules."

Group organizations, in sum, bound men together into relationships within which they subsequently formulated rules that enforced rights and duties, liberties and obligations, germane to the proper conduct of their varying interests.

20

Power and Relationships in Institutions

THROUGH early informal rules (unwritten codes, folkways, customary practices that become common law) and from these to the elaborate legal codes of states and empires, organizations canalize human behavior. First within each respective association and then across the lines within which are other men in different associations, organized groups induce, exact, or otherwise obtain desired conduct from constituent or external individuals. The individual thereby finds his own capacity to act expanded and liberated but, by the same token, at times circumscribed or controlled.

But how, essentially, does the group actually force men to act by the rules, to conform to patterns of right or desired conduct? To condition behavior, each organization exerts some form of power. Power, in its turn, thereby emerges as an intrinsic attribute of organizations, informal or formal, large or small. Encompassing the inducements, sanctions, or punishments by which the group enforces conformity to rights and duties within and across the lines of association, the organization represents *purposeful* power. For Commons, that adjective once more stressed man's volition in economic action, and distinguished social power from "blind" power, i.e., from the energies of nature which man also harnesses for his ends.

Kinds and Degrees of Power

If power constitutes an earmark of all social organization, any single institution may be differentiated from others by the kind and degree of power it can invoke. Three major types may be recognized:

At the top of the hierarchy stands *sovereign* power, the power of government. Sovereignty manifestly connotes the possession and exercise of supreme power within a given society. For government can enforce its regulations in the final analysis by physical sanctions—freedom or imprisonment, withholding and granting use of property, power over life and death.

Next must be ranked *economic* power, the power lodged, for instance, in corporations and unions. They exact desired behavior from individuals by utilizing the availability or scarcity of jobs, materials, labor, and other focal attributes of ownership. Economic power corresponds to the legal concept of "coercion," as distinguished from the "duress" available to the sovereign power of government.

A third category of power may be termed *moral*. This is the power that is characteristic of religious, philanthropic, fraternal, communal, and professional associations. As differentiated from duress and coercion, the inducements by which this last type of institution exacts conformity stem mainly from the pull of shared loyalties, sentiments, and traditions.

But, if group power may thus be usefully differentiated, in everyday social living, power lines actually follow no sharply separate courses. We can readily trace for ourselves various—and typically revealing—linkages in the current networks of power. Moral power, for instance, is manifestly not the exclusive prerogative of those institutions which cannot exercise physical or economic power as such. Corporations and unions, institutions chiefly of economic power, seek to persuade the community that their programs serve the public interest.

Governments, the sovereign powers, also invoke moral sentiments. Totalitarian dictatorships—the most ruthless power units of our day—make constant and, indeed, monopolistic use of the propaganda of self-righteousness. They stand forth, in fact, not only as the most iron-curtained propagandists but also as the most iron-voiced. In democratic American society, on the other hand, though power lines blur one into the other, checks and balances continue to function by the sheer vitality of independent group activity. Moreover, the capacity for enforcement remains an ordered legal hierarchy of sanctions. Government exercises its physical compulsions only as "last resorts"—and then within a frame of explicit working rules involving due process. Beyond that, corporations and unions are under pressure to keep within an orbit of the "rule of reason."

Effect on Individuals

These realities of purposeful power establish the potency of social or group relationships. For if power to enforce desired modes of conduct must be exercised within structured relationships, the relationships themselves become important components in action. Man is actually individualized, in one sense, by all the groups that exercise their diverse and respective powers over him to canalize his everyday life activities. He becomes himself a system of relations and an institutionalized personality as he absorbs the cumulating layers of patterned responses, characteristic of groups of which he is a member, into the personal individuality that belongs to his own character as a human being.

In sum, relationships, through multiple rights and duties accepted by the individual as a member of his society and enforced by varying group powers, are the characteristic channels of behavior in the economy, and the web of influences by which individual *action* is not only controlled but also liberated and expanded.

Transactions and Bargains

Thus structure and action remain related from the outset. The study of "collective action," of man-in-his-economy, may permit the separation of one from the other for analytical purposes. But clearly it does not prove possible to maintain for long any separation of *action* by the group from *structure* of the group. Fully to understand our "going concerns," we must proceed immediately from exploration of their character as "concerns" to trace the modes of their "going." Then as we follow "action" step by step through its manifold ramifications in industrial society, we finally discover why administration has been steadily proving itself so central a process of our functioning economy.

In the analysis of economic action, Commons proposed the transaction as the smallest observable unit of economic activity, in place of the "exchange" of traditional economics. By so doing, he sought to mirror in his basic components of action the whole collective structure of the economy. As might be expected, moreover, Commons's "transaction" stresses the group, instead of the individual, as the prime agent in economic choice, decision, and activity. Although it constitutes the smallest unit for observation, every transaction involves a minimum of five persons, in contrast with the simple buyer-seller axis of the exchange. It involves the two people completing any effective economic action; at least two more who had been most closely considered as possible alternatives (one each for the two primary participants); and a fifth party available, even if not used, as an impartial judge to resolve disputes regarding the rights and duties of the transactors under the relevant working rules applicable to the activity they were completing together.

A universe of transactions offers an analytical advantage over the older concept of the market. It facilitates differentiation of the three types of activities actually characterizing our modern economy: bargaining, managerial, and rationing transactions. Each type is distinguished from the other—again paralleling the structures of organized groups—by the kind of powers they can invoke to obtain mutual observance of reciprocal rights and obligations essential for carrying the transaction to its proper completion.

Only within the *bargaining* transaction, most recent in economic evolution, do transactors deal one with the other as equals. The parties may be individual men, or they may be billion-dollar corporations and million-member unions. But they meet and deal together as legal equals, free to determine by their own choice whether to assume the obligations of the proposed bargain at the price set and in the quantities stipulated under the conditions proposed. Against the "other side," each can seek better terms by recognized recourses like the strike or the lockout or by other means, if available. But once the bargain has been completed, duties are recognized in exchange for equally recognized and supposedly equivalent rights that are reciprocally enforceable.

This setup differentiates bargaining from managerial and rationing transactions, where the parties not only do not deal as legal equals but simply cannot so deal if the functions embraced in these transactions are to be effectively carried out.

Despite all the modifications that have been made over the years, the *managerial* transaction remains today an evolution of the historic master-servant relationship. Even in a mass-production plant, where a supervisory agent of a multibranched corporation works with the employee members of a national union, production cannot proceed unless the supervisor can give relevant orders which the employee must obey. (The newly won right to protest under defined contractual conditions comes later.) The superior-subordinate relation on the job may not be described with the invidious old words of master-servant or superior-inferior, but it continues to comprise the same basic realities. For the legal—and technical—chain of command remains inherent in the allocations of responsibilities.

Just so, the *rationing* transaction, encompassing perhaps a still older form of essential economic activity, implies the lodging of power to make decisions, and enforce them, in a superior authority. Government determination of fiscal needs, against which taxes and other assessments are recurrently levied, represents the most familiar example. Modern corporation executives carry forward parallel rationing transactions when they determine expenditures that must be balanced against potential gross income and apportion actual income among those with the legal title to share it.

Evolution of Bargaining Transactions

In all present-day economies, transactions are to be understood only as products of continuous development, with power and relationships as the chief threads of their progressive evolution. By eliminating the whole category of bargaining transactions, for instance, while returning rationing and management transactions exclusively to the state, fascist and communist economies prove themselves to be regressions to more primitive stages of society. In Anglo-American society, in contrast, strong evolutionary threads have been noticeable. For instance, our great documents from the Magna Carta to the Bill of Rights (and thereafter) chart the gradual decentralization of sovereign power achieved through the checks interposed by groups of free men and the new balances created among the multiplying groups—winning recognized rights and accepting fresh duties.

Another thread emerges from the customs and laws that modified the feudal rent bargain into the capitalist price bargain and finally into the wage bargain. The changes in types of bargains have followed closely expansions in the legal definitions of property:

1. In the feudal economy, men conceived of property in terms of physical things—legal property which the courts termed *corporeal.* The rights of ownership in such real property com-

prised the right to use them oneself and to prevent trespass by others. With these inherent rights went ordered relations for working the land and allocating the products.

2. As time went on, physical resources and tangibles retained their significance, but obligations to pay negotiable debts—the type of property the law distinguished as *incorporeal*—also had become highly important articles of practical exchange and so proper subjects for legally recognized rights and duties within the domain of property ownership. Indeed, the right to convert debts (obligations incurred in the past) into negotiable articles of present exchange ranks as one of man's great social inventions.

3. Finally, claims to future or expected earning power also became articles of present exchange—property rights that can be owned, acquired, transferred. They now constitute the *intangible* property recognized by broadening legal definition, including rights to income anticipated from business good will, trademarks, corporate stocks, and patents.

The network of relationships and powers encompassed within the "wage bargain" has been going through an evolution roughly parallel with these legal changes, with the most dramatic chapter written in this country. The surviving institution of slavery maintained one form of labor as *corporeal* property in the United States even as industrialization was transforming the economy; the physical person of the slave could be bought and sold like any other commodity of commerce. Indenture and then peonage suggested rather a category of *incorporeal* property, in that the obligation to give labor for a defined period represented a debt owed by the laborer. Today the free wage bargain resembles most closely the transactions concerned with *intangible* property rights, since the employer now acquires with his promise to pay wages the expected future labor of his employee, to be expended under stated conditions at the agreed rate.

The job transaction thus emerges, in a sense, the most complex and subtle of all transactions, because its conduct, considerations, and completion never can be really separated from the persons of the transactors. Yet, under our constitutional guarantees against involuntary servitude, the employer has no legally enforceable claim upon the labor of his employee. The employee, for his part, in selling his labor sells a continuing promise to obey commands in those managerial transactions in which he participates to produce goods and services. This promise is not legally enforceable, whereas the employer's reciprocal promise to pay wages for such labor becomes a debt upon his business. Beyond question, the essential outcome of this proliferating wage bargain yields to the modern free employee, in his labor power, property rights that are both incorporeal and intangible—but no longer in any way corporeal. For his physical person can never be attached, not even when he withholds collectively and invalidly through a wildcat strike the labor power he has contracted to sell.

The present-day wage bargain, finally, often assimilates the many transactions projected by a larger bargain between institutional equals. Within the framework of collective bargaining contracts negotiated by labor unions and corporations, rules covering far more than wages are established and administered to impinge upon the whole complex of managing, rationing, and bargaining transactions by which goods are produced in present-day industry. In these major economic organizations, indeed, all three types of transactions appear within each group structure and intermesh across them all. Worker and employer engage in bargaining transactions to determine under what conditions labor power is to be expended at given rates in jobs. Those very same jobs are from day to day directed by means of managerial transactions. At the same time, corporate income is rationed by executives even as they face union officials pressing for a larger share in the whole "take" through defined forms of returns and benefits.

Thus it is that transactions have generated new concepts of property, of economic relations, and of economic dealings, progressively fitted to evolving American practice. Nor has a terminal point been reached in the process of continuing adjustments between rights and duties, between thought and practice, within the framework of the three classes of transactions. On the contrary, the pressures continue, each group of organized individuals demanding new rights and resisting new demands from the other.

21

Conflict, Mutuality, and Resolution

THE process of change that has expanded the content of basic transactions has not just happened. People have made it come to pass. Changing conditions of economic life certainly have furnished the first spur to new adjustments. But the human beings continuously engaged in transactions have forged the specific adaptations, the new ways of behaving, in the changing economy.

Pressures and counterpressures are exerted on transactors as men seek to promote their own interests, goals, and objectives. The pushing and pulling between the parties variously at interest—employer and employee, buyer and seller, taxpayer and tax collector, corporation director and corporation stockholder, and all the other familiar juxtapositions—give transactions three behavioral links: conflict, mutuality, and resolution. By such linked modes of behaving, transactions are carried forward, and the resolutions of conflict generate both immediate settlements and long-term adaptations to change.

Behavioral Links

Conflict emerges an enduring and omnipresent reality in all economic behavior, because one man's right proves the other man's duty, one transactor's interest becomes the other's obligation, and—even more fundamentally—because the natural world, from which we must draw so many materials essential to human living, imposes limitations of scarcity upon its satisfactions. And even as we master more techniques toward achieving the abundant society, in the here and now we always face scarcity in terms of man's desires and wants all over the globe. We still have not been able to increase man-hour productivity even in America beyond 2½ to 3 per cent per annum.

Yet, because the group remains always immanent in transactions and because economic activity equates with human interacting, mutuality and interdependence are also inescapable. Men may start with conflicts of interest, of rights and duties, but the completion of any transaction is sought precisely because all stand to gain by its effectuation. Moreover, the continuously improving technical equipment provided by the application of science to production—the principle of efficiency—places abundance, even in a world of limited natural resources, within the reach of social man.

But precisely because transactions are thus conditioned both by scarce opportunities and the potential of increasingly "efficient" abundance, the men involved in those transactions need some instruments, some resources by which they can project, carry forward, and complete their transactions in orderly fashion, resolving conflict by jointly accepted rules and promoting mutuality by recognized rights and duties. The methods by which interacting human beings achieve agreement and mutually satisfactory valuations in such complex situations, rooted in genuine conflicts of interest, remain always the ultimate test of any society.

Within this generic pattern, conflict at any given time may appear baffling and weakening to the democratic way of life. But, despite the seeming babel of clashing claims and counsels, conflict is an integral element of growth, of progressive and continuous adjustment. It forges the first link in a chain by which men seek pragmatically "the best practical thing to do (in successive situations) under the actual circumstances of conflicting economic interests."

The second link, however, must not be obscured by the more dramatic aspects of conflicts. In the end, dealings among transactors must serve the interests of both sides. Accordingly, conflicts are never far removed from interdependencies. Mutuality, in a word, coexists with conflict in every transaction, because in the end no party can serve his interest without action by his opposite number.

Obviously, buyers can be actual buyers only when they face sellers, workers can be actual workers only when they produce goods under managers, and so on. At some point, they fix the terms of settlement which will resolve conflict and promote mutuality. Thereby the completion of every transaction projects not only an orderly resolution of conflict but also agreement upon the locus of effective mutuality. After conflicts have been faced and handled, and then obligations mutually accepted and performed, a working principle of order becomes a third dimension, so to speak, of the intrinsic qualities of every transaction.

Achieving Order

The achievement of order, however, is itself a complex matter. It involves not only the transacting individuals but also the rules which they accept for defining respective rights and obligations. These rules comprise many forms of controls: the various regulations by which every association holds its constituents to its own code of behavior, standards formulated and agreed upon between organized groups, and the law of the land.

Within this framework, parties at interest may achieve a working settlement themselves. Before such terms of settlement are agreed upon, some recourse to power may occur as, for instance, a strike. But strikes themselves are subject to mutually formulated and accepted rules. Thus both valid strikes (at the expiration of contracts) and invalid stoppages (during the term of contract) are differentiated in collective agreements.

In the same way, by prior rule, the parties are not limited to relying entirely on recourse to power for achieving resolution, nor indeed are they always permitted to take such a course. A third party may be called in, or may take the initiative in intervening. Third-party intervention, as a matter of practice, may be integrated into the transaction, as when parties agree to refer differences to arbitration.

This built-in principle of order inherent in transactions, finally, makes it possible for society to advance by peaceful evolution as against violent revolution. It provides an established method, so to speak, for adapting working rules to changing circumstance.

Negotiational Psychology

If the *individual-in-action* emerges as a transactor interacting with other men, if he functions mainly through organized groups, no economics can nevertheless merely bypass this individual as man and at the same time claim title to completely adequate insights for interpreting economic activity.

Although the human being in his economy does not act wholly by rational calculation, he does in economic action balance means and ends, instruments and goals, more volitionally than in many other orbits of daily living. Thus this individual-in-action must be seen in the image of his institutional setting.

Each man's work includes specific tasks and functions within an ordered sector of the economy; these tasks become by that very token then also a link in behavior with other men to make individual man an institutionalized personality, a member of groups. Psychological analysis must be applied not only to the division of labor and division of function that bind each man to his fellows but also to the characteristic behavior of negotiation, of give and take, of conciliation, of the resolution of dispute by which all together get done the daily work of their world.

Certainly men-in-action respond to many influences beyond the motivating sources of their transactions. But economists must be mainly concerned with the inducements and considerations that lead individuals to behave as they do with each other in producing, rationing, and exchanging goods and services. Economists must focus on the drives that create conflicts in transactions, that impart consciousness of mutuality, and that promote orderly resolutions.

Individual action of this sort does not proceed sheerly from inner compulsions; external factors play their part. Motivation thus becomes a pattern of inner and outer stimuli and response. The individual makes a choice in every transaction from among available alternatives and, by that token, also avoids rejected courses; he performs an agreed or compelled action; and finally, he may forbear from exercising the full degree of power which he is capable of exerting to direct or exact the given act. Such forbearance is exemplified in the complex chain of motivation that makes employers deem it good business policy not to drive employees too hard or that leads a union leader to safeguard employment by keeping wage demands at a lower level than might be immediately enforceable.

This power of the human *will-in-action* distinguishes it among all natural forces. Performance, avoidance, forbearance—here are the dimensions of characteristic behavior in transactions by which the individual acts like a sane adult with a will and a purpose.

But just what is he—this sane adult individual, this will-in-action within the economy? Manifestly, what we need is a social psychology of negotiational, transactional man.

Time Dimensions

The problems of individual motivation must thus be returned ultimately to their social grounding. Only then can we gain meaningful insight into their significant time dimension. For it is from the social conditioning of all human experience that the past exerts its continuing influence—through the channeling of custom, law, training, and all the rules and routines cumulated over the generations. The future impinges upon the present through men's hopes and plans and purposes for things still to come for themselves and their descendents.

But how exactly do anticipated results motivate men to make choices that often involve satisfactions in the future? The problem of "futurity" has long been avoided by economists, because it appears to make effect precede cause—a sequence contrary to that established by the natural sciences. The answer once again is found in the group nature of economic action. Social institutions and group organizations assure continuities and thus give men a "security of expectancies" that permits them to base current action upon anticipated effects.

More specifically, group organizations crystallize all past experience as the customs and routines that shape present action. They frame working rules to formalize such past experience, to guide present action, and to set forth accepted definitions regarding rights and duties. They guarantee the future achievement of results from present action, measurable by present expectations regarding the future and then enforceable in the future by the accepted rules carried forward from the past. Institutions and organized groups, in short, are the time binders.

Working Rules

Working rules, then, manifestly constitute pervasive and crucial instruments of group purpose and action. They have proved themselves the prime tools of adaptation through the various regulations formulated by men in their institutional life to exact desired behavior from individuals.

They include, in the first instance when association is still in the informal stage, deep-rooted, unwritten common-law precepts, folkways, or codes, defining behavior expected by all from each.

With formalization of the group association, these folkways and codes attain various explicit and concrete embodiments which make the working rules enforceable mandates of the common will. Working rules, thereupon, take the form of legislative statutes, judicial decisions, and administrative orders of the state; policies, decisions, and regulations of corporations; constitutions, convention decisions, rules of unions; business contracts, collective bargaining agreements, arbitral decisions, and so on.

But, although working rules thus represent in their origins a tool and instrument of the social group—of men acting in association—they also make any organization more than a sum of its constituent individuals. As the social cement binding each individual with his group and the group with its social past and future, the working rules, like the organizations of which they are a part, transcend any present institutional setup. Precisely by changes in the working rules, alternative courses become available to provide adaptation to changing conditions.

The chain of influence is, however, circular, so that, if the working rules make the organization more than its immediate constituency, the constituents must make and adaptively change the working rules. We cannot stop with the generalization—important though it remains in itself—that each organization adds up to more than a sum of its member-individuals, or even that it represents something different from an "abstract entity" or a cumulation of working rules.

We must recognize also that social organization remains a human device that must be operated by men; its aims and rules and stores of tradition are vitalized by each current roster of members who administer or change the rules to carry out the underlying constitution.

Administrative Procedures

Administratively, Commons's projected association may be seen as a three-level arrangement, within which the top leaders maintain their contacts with the rank and file through a small intermediate group of "activists." The men in the ranks seldom keep continuous check on the command or leadership, and vice versa.

Just as Commons had found in judicial interpretation of corporation law the term "going concern" for the group organization itself, so he found in union administration a term for that "activist" minority which formed the transmission belt, the line of communication, in every organization between leaders and constituency. When a new course of action was contemplated, Commons observed that the salaried officials of a union were wont to say, "Get the *activity* together and see how they will take it." The "activity" designated the "organization staff workers, that part of the 'rank and file' which attended meetings, reported on the sentiment of its members, and with the elected leaders formulated the policies of the union and established the collective agreements with their employers."

The "activity" was figured at about 10 per cent of the total membership. Commons appropriated the term for general use, since his own experience substantiated the findings of so many different social investigators regarding the omnipresence of this minority elite. He saw the "activity" as the party workers in the political machine, the management team in a corporation, the administration stalwarts in the union local, and so on. The leaders, with the "activity," constituted the effective agents for adapting the working rules to changing conditions.

Thus it is that although the corporate institution has a life of its own and transcends the generations through its working rules that carry past to present and facilitate advance from present to future, only through the administrative procedures by which its current constituency makes each association go, do the working rules and organization program provide these continuities.

This means also, however, that no organization ever exists apart from its constituency. Neither the leaders nor the activity can "personify" the organization; nor can the organization become more than organized people by the majesty of the capital letter that transforms a government into a State, a union into Labor, a corporation into Enterprise.

Instead, as a safeguard for individual liberty, it is always well to remember that at any given time the state remains *politicians-in-action;* the union, *labor-officials-in-action;* and the corporation, *business-executives-in-action.* Each of these collectives simply carries out the expected and promised behavior by which duties are enforced and liberties safeguarded.

Even before our own day of semantic sophistication, Commons warned against confusing "the compass with the ocean." In the heated discussions over conflicting interests and policy making, we easily load words with value judgments, conflicting loyalities, powerful sentiments. But reality remains infinitely more human, complex, pluralistic, and specifically social than any such stereotypes as "Wall Street," "statism," or "labor monopoly" would signify. So long as the state, for instance, remains simply the currently elected politicians-in-action, so long as citizen members retain the right to change the working rules by which action is shaped, they are not a mere mass of atomistic individuals confronting their total government.

Power to enforce collective rules remains always the instrument of ordering society. But whether it is concentrated in one dominant institution or divided among multiple organizations, whether it is centralized or decentralized along sectors recognizedly sovereign, economic, or moral—these are the questions that determine the measure of freedom man enjoys. For freedom, too, is a social creation before it becomes a natural right.

Within such a context—the Western democratic context—working rules remain tools of human purposes, pervasive yet diverse, liberating yet controlling. Within each institution they embody the duties and, thus, the controls imposed upon member individuals by the collective action of all decreeing together. Across organization frontiers they define the rights and immunities reciprocally recognized.

Just as working rules are generated by all the social procedures in the group—that is, not only by legislation but also by administration, executive action, arbitration, conciliation, and sheer crystallizing custom—so they are changed as changing circumstance requires new adjustments. The settlement of disputes and conflicts in past transactions yields the rules or precedents for guiding present activities; the current rules, as guarantees of future expected behavior, yield tests of their own adequacy in unfolding practical situations.

22

Administration as a Key

WORKING rules do not in themselves, however, make for ordered and sound relationships, especially as society grows increasingly complex and large. Certainly it remains always important that each organization retains the right to change its own working rules, that none arrogates to itself all powers to condition individual behavior. When these internal safeguards are provided, however, the interacting of the many large but still decentralized and independent collectives must now increasingly be supplemented by machinery for administration.

A New Pattern

Such administration, in Commons's concept, would provide a new pattern of adaptation to change. He saw, for instance, the prosecuting agency of regulatory law transformed into a staff of experts, cooperating with executives of corporations, unions, and other economic organizations to find solutions for new problems. He also saw that advisory committees, chosen from interest groups, might negotiate acceptable standards of action for government to enforce.

Commons became interested in this phase of administration during the early years of the century when the movement for enacting workmen's compensation laws got under way. Prior to these laws the courts applied the common-law rules of negligence to determine liability after accidents had happened. This procedure resulted, in the main, in exonerating employers from responsibility. Even in the occasional cases where employer liability was found, supervisory officials often were penalized. This, Commons felt, misread the institutional character of business as well as the challenge of high accident rates.

Commons also found himself impressed, in the course of an investigation of the steel industry, with the developing program of safety work. The corporations were placing emphasis on safety engineers to save costs by preventing accidents rather than on lawyers to avert legal liability. He saw a fruitful clue in this record. Could not representatives of industry and of labor be appointed to advisory boards and, under the guidance of safety engineers, formulate codes based upon the best experience already prevailing? Could not accident compensation laws thus be focused on improving daily functions rather than on assessing fault, on preventing accidents even more than on compensating for them?

Experiments in Wisconsin with industrial administration, in which he participated, yielded what seemed to him a promising approach toward promoting such progressive yet practical controls. They demonstrated that, if the changing nature of the economy requires adaptive programs for meeting ever-new, specific problems of central importance to economic interest groups as well as to the whole community, two types of program were available:

1. Such problems as accidents, unemployment, and sickness can be met as they were at first by assessing blame and, perhaps, prosecuting particular parties against whom defined responsibilities might be lodged. But this way seldom proves the only—or the best—way.

2. Far better is it to meet these problems by setting up objective safeguards than by identifying subjective culprits.

These safeguards, however, must meet three rigorous tests: (*a*) they must be in practical enough form to be translated into workaday realities; (*b*) they must appear fair to reasonable men; (*c*) they must stand forth as progressive and be based on accomplishments already registered that establish the proposed advance as achievable standard practice.

Interorganizational Function

In terms of such tests, the role of administrators should be to serve an interorganizational function. Precisely because government administrators have been multiplying so rapidly, Commons felt it urgent to define their function as supplementary rather than dominating. That is why he came to deplore so insistently all tendencies that made government agents prosecutors of "violations" rather than experts helping the parties at interest to develop sound practices.

He would achieve, rather, a type of tripartite administration —through the appointment of advisory committees that would bring together around the government agency (like the Industrial Commission of Wisconsin) practical spokesmen for the interests concerned. These spokesmen could then hammer out through negotiation a code of good and acceptable practices for each problem before them.

Such a code could be defended before the courts as conforming with "due process" and the "rule of reason" better than one devised completely by legislators and imposed, in turn, by inspectors. Commons had witnessed the process in Wisconsin, as already indicated, where employers established mutual insurance companies, which, in their turn, hired the former factory inspectors to serve as safety engineers. Thus conflicts were avoided, mutuality was promoted, and orderly progress toward the goal of reducing accidents was achieved.

Commons was troubled for some time with the problem of drafting, within such an operating framework for administration, standards both reasonable and progressive, rather than mere compromises on successive needs at the point of the average practice. It was with the excitement of real discovery that he worked out with his colleagues the formula which took for the criteria of "reasonable" not the average but the *best* practices already effectively enforced in an economic area. Thus a target was set in cooperation with practitioners themselves, at which they all might reasonably be expected to aim, and which thus projected general future improvement upon best current achievement.

Third-party Intervention

But how about conflicts which the parties themselves fail to resolve? How about disputes that arise when the rules evolved by one group infringe upon another, when differences crystallize over the intermeshing lines of reciprocal rights and duties, immunities, and responsibilities? Here, too, the same administrative pattern, in Commons's system of thought, furnishes the machinery for ordered resolutions. "Third parties" may then be called in to interpret rules, settle differences, apply the group intent to the concrete situation. The arbitrator, the expert, the impartial expounder of the law above men, all can and do operate under procedures that effectuate changes in the rules, as well as interpret them.

Voluntary bargaining can thus be supplemented by varying interventions—if and where need be. Such procedures then become themselves part of organized relationships on the familiar model of "due process" in Anglo-American law. They provide the means by which the rules of individual and group action can be changed peacefully—by gradual progressive evolution, rather than by disruptive total revolution—precisely because they afford the essential alternative of "order" instead of disagreement.

Admittedly, pressures for changing underlying working rules, and resistances against such pressures, create some of our sharpest intergroup conflicts. Here, therefore, evolving administration on the Commons pattern performs a most vital function. For, in Commons's view, economic working rules are most soundly changed when disinterested administrators help practitioners—parties at interest—discover the reasonable, practical thing to do, which at the same time marks the progressive step forward.

Strategic Timing

By the whole inner logic of this analysis, human experience in society proves itself an endless *becoming*. Time stands forth as an integral part of the social process—and, in the long perspective of American experience, a heartening part. Man's affairs are always social, and "social affairs are also relative to time." Social processes, historic uniformities and diversities, emerge from time itself, and in planning, willing, acting, and thinking, man shows this conditioning imprint of his society from the flow of time.

But man remains still the planful, volitional actor in social and economic affairs; man has choices and, by making them, exercises his human influence in channeling the same continuing flow of events along one available course rather than another. If past experience entered into the motivations by which men acted in the century behind us, not only as human beings in the age of industrialization but also as Americans or Russians or Frenchmen, future events will be similarly anticipated in choices men severally make today.

It is not hard to see the factors that limit such choices; what needs to be stressed increasingly is the area within which human decisions can exercise *strategic* influence. In our own society that area remains relatively wide, both for the individual and for his multiple organizations. But the requirements of right and skillful action also become ever more exacting and challenging, precisely as the complexities of large-scale activities multiply.

Routine versus Strategic Decisions

Every leader confronts from day to day a succession of "routine transactions" in which he must nonetheless make effective decisions. Now and then, also, he will confront a transaction that will prove truly strategic, because what he does in it will control a significant chain of consequences. He must be able to recognize such controlling, or strategic, transactions; he must be able to recognize the limiting factor through which, as administrator, he can seek to control each situation before relinquishing it to routine.

Just as a farmer on his acres needs to know when to supply potash in raising his crops, and in what quantities, and at what point in his chain of production; just so the corporation manager faces strategic actions in his chain of producing, pricing, and marketing goods; just so the administrator in the Federal Reserve System, in his turn, confronts comparable questions—on changing the rediscount rate, for instance, to grapple with inflation or deflation; and just so the labor leader must be able to recognize the controlling factors—on formulating bargaining demands, for example.

Reduced to the homely examples of concrete daily action in the American economy, the requirements seem familiar, even simple. Yet they spell out the content of effective administration in our total economy; they justify the generalization that, if time constitutes social process, timeliness in economic action and policy making—a sense of timing—constitutes the social skill of administrative control.*

* It is interesting to compare Commons's concepts of strategic transaction, negotiational psychology, and administrative "timeliness" with the more recent economic discussions based upon John von Neumann and Oskar Morgenstern, *Theory of Games and Economic Behavior*, 2d ed., Princeton University Press, Princeton, N.J., 1947; see also the useful popularization by John McDonald, *Strategy in Poker, Business and War*, W. W. Norton & Company, Inc., New York, 1950. For a later treatment of the same subject, see Robert Duncan Luce and Howard Raiffa, *Games and Decisions*, John Wiley & Sons, Inc., New York, 1957.

Commons recognized that he was advancing no new principle here, that businessmen long had ranked "timing" high among the requirements of effective policy. But he assimilated the principle into the context of transactions and through these transactions also into man's controls over his social direction. He thus required in the daily job of every economic practitioner skills that connected it with the organized policy making of every group association. Finally, he gave significant dimensions to administrative skill. It is no longer enough to know *what* to do. Leaders must know also *when* to do it and *to what extent.* Timeliness marks off the strategic transaction from the routine, the one that proves controlling from the one that does not; it expands administrative skills thereby into the skills of social control.

As of the present, this capacity of knowing "just when, how much, and under what circumstances" still belongs to the realm of genius or, as some of us would say, to a sort of intuition. "The general principles of timeliness and strategy," Commons held, may be pointed out but "can never be reduced to a science." Yet there remains a safeguard—and a recompense. If the skill may not become "scientific" in the accepted sense of the word, if we must continue to rely on managerial know-how or administrative experience rather than the predictable precisions of causation, science gives way to administrative talent precisely because at any given moment the future looms undetermined. Only the past is set and finished; each current generation can leave its mark upon the shape of things to come.

In Conclusion

Here then, in the economics Commons offered, is distilled an analysis of action in modern industry, an exploration of the mechanisms by which men in their group relations seek answers to ever-new problems amid ever-changing practical realities. There emerges essentially, therefore, a guide for administrators, a method for approaching and handling problems rather than any set of fixed or final solutions to them.

To be sure, Commons's theory already needs correction by (or, shall we say, adjustment to) unfolding events. Implicit in his thinking is a conviction of almost automatic beneficence in the institutions he describes—an internal beneficence arising from their expansion of the individual's capacity for freedom and effectiveness; an external beneficence generated by the positive results for the whole community from bargaining and negotiation, with the checks and balances upon organized group power they automatically call into play as corporations and unions deal together, within a manifold web of working rules and with a minimum of breakdown, to yield freedoms at a price reasonable for the community.

Perhaps Commons would have been less confident concerning these potentialities had his experience and study continued into the recent period of nationwide collective bargaining. We shall examine presently some of the problems he did not foresee, particularly union developments. Perhaps too, he might have redefined the potentialities of administration as that "fourth branch of government" which promised orderly progress, had he been able to observe the proliferation of government agencies in recent years, had he continued to be as closely the *participant* observer as he had been in the experience of decades before. Perhaps he would have seen that the administrative agency in government does not so easily mediate the power tug as it yields a measure of ground to the more powerful groups at any given time.

As it stands, Commons's work, for all his perceptiveness and perspicacity, exhibits a highly revealing example of the inevitable impress made upon every man by his time and its problems. If Commons saw the business corporation in historic perspective as the strategic instrument of human purpose that it has been in democratic industrial society, he observed that instrument in its first power thrust, when labor organization was weak and government's dominant policies were cast in the philosophy of minimum intervention. By the same perspective, he could feel that a better balance of group power, when unions would bargain as equals with corporations, would yield inevitably beneficent improvements; that state action, complementing such voluntarism and proceeding with the participation of parties-at-interest, would promote the general welfare.

But the first manifestations of the new dispensation have not altogether squared with the forecasts. Now that it is organized labor which has been functioning in its first power thrust, while the state increases its interventions, we can see that mediation of the power tugs does not follow as directly as Commons—with many others—believed it would when group power had achieved better balance. Nor did he measure adequately the opposite side of the group power coin which made the prized individual freedoms of the American industrial citizen themselves a social creation before they were natural rights.

We may agree with Commons that modern American society is a complex network of group organizations, each of which expands, liberates, and controls individual action. But the controls raise problems that are not obviated by the concomitant liberations and expansions. That is why we are becoming increasingly aware that the individual must possess established safeguards against the powers vested, however essentially, in all the groups through which he functions.

For we who follow Commons are seeing ever more clearly that, if he lived in a day in which it proved necessary to affirm the place and significance of the group in our individualistic America, we, the successor generations, face again the challenge of safeguarding the individual's rights and personality against the multiple powerful group pressures closing in upon him. Nor can we, who reject with Commons the older faith that the free man's pursuit of self-interest adds up automatically to general welfare, feel that the untrammeled interaction of powerful interest organizations adds up automatically to socially responsible action.

Yet these questions do not prove incompatible with the theory Commons offered for understanding the dynamics of American enterprise. For he accepted the reality that problems continuously arise. He also projected a framework, not for their solution, it should be noted, but for their resolution. Indeed, the savor of familiar reality and characteristic experience emanates from Commons's pages. Perhaps his major contribution to us lies in his impressively documented demonstration that the crucial group organizations of our society—the corporation, the union, the democratic state—represent, as it were, great human or social inventions. They are interrelated inventions, no one of which can long endure without the others.

No immediate difficulties, therefore, should jolt us into attacks that weaken any valid group associations. Nor need we recoil before the apparently incessant conflicts among them; this struggle is part of the bargaining among *equals*. But interdependence is also part of the bargaining process; it is intrinsic in economic action, intrinsic as are, too, the mechanisms for orderly settlements and adaptations to changing conditions.

Because Commons thus remained always concerned with these dynamics of adjustment among organized equals, rather than with fixed or final answers to any of their incessantly pressing problems, his economics offers basic concepts from which we, his successors, can take up where he left off. For in his insistence upon method for administrative thinking, administrative action, and administrative adaptation—creative, progressive, realistic administration, predicated always upon the best achievements in practical everyday relationships and industrial experience—there lies the key for uncovering workable answers to problems that never end among men in society.

PART VI

Wanted: a Moral Framework

23

Justice and the New Constitutionalism

HAVING pointed out possible pitfalls in the new posture of moral and social responsibility assumed by business during the past quarter of a century—the danger of cynicism and self-righteousness, at one extreme and, at the other, the danger of perfectionism or assuming too great a moral burden—it is appropriate to ask what aspect of morality *should* be emphasized and implemented by business.

What one should expect and, indeed, demand of business, in my opinion, is justice. Management must so organize its corporate operation as to ensure justice to the various individuals and groups associated with the enterprise. This is no small assignment. To do justice requires a type of constitutionalism—the time-honored means by which societies have put checks on power so as to protect rights and interests. Yet history is replete with the difficulties experienced in drafting constitutions. Many of the questions that political leaders have debated will need to be pondered in similar form by businessmen. For instance, is it a written constitution that we want for corporations, or an unwritten one? Or should it be partly written and partly unwritten? Shall we provide for the three typical branches of constitutional government, namely, legislative, executive, and judicial? And what about a bill of rights, which is part and parcel of every modern constitution to safeguard inalienable liberties? Again, how can we safeguard the interests of the people depending upon the corporate activity without putting too many restrictions on the executive's capacity to function not only as an effective administrator but also as an innovator and enterpriser?

Just to pose these questions indicates how difficult it may be to work out an appropriate constitutionalism to govern corporate life. And yet, without some form of constitutionalism, all the talk about moral and social responsibility may become meaningless. For a corporation is essentially a power system. It organizes economic power through capital, machinery, labor, materials, and merchandising. Management has it within its power to offer or withhold jobs, to make available or withhold commodities or service to the community, to buy or refuse to buy materials from suppliers, to utilize different modes of transportation—railway, waterway, air, trucks. All these together constitute power of major importance to those involved directly *and* indirectly in corporate activity.

Since, in a legal sense at least, the corporation is organized to yield profits, all these powers may be invoked to maximize profits to the neglect of other functions, such as serving the community, respecting the dignity of all those engaged in the enterprise, or maintaining decent conditions of work. Moreover, since the executive is faced with the usual temptations bestrewing the path of those to whom great power is committed, there is always the danger that he will misuse his authority.

Indeed, rarely in history has a group of men been given such unlimited power as is now enjoyed by executives of large corporations. Ownership has become diffuse and impersonal. A few men—top operating managers and sometimes a few members of the board of directors—control the typical firm. Constantly confronted in the conduct of business with the dilemma of "the technical *must* versus the ethical *ought*," they tend naturally to favor the former. Prudence weights the scales on the side of conserving property interests, even when it means laying off people, reducing wages, or moving a plant from one part of the country to another, in spite of the devastation overtaking the old community.

Lesson of Constitutionalism

An examination of an extensive latter-day development of constitutionalism may serve to guide our thinking as well as give caution against expecting any easy road to achieving justice. I am referring to the large-scale growth of collective bargaining during the past quarter-century. The development of constitutionalism is not always a benign and peaceful process. Nor is the attempt to endow a new group with power—necessary as it may be to establish a better balance—without its dangerous potential of abuse and corruption. For example, we know that constitutions not infrequently result from acts of revolt, as in the case of the Magna Carta or the Declaration of Independence and the American Constitution. And in the later stages, when romanticism and idealism wear off, the problem becomes one of preventing the misuse of power.

It should not be surprising, therefore, that violence attended the rise of constitutionalism in American industry. Here was indeed a situation of revolt. Trade unions, unable for decades to secure a foothold in the heart of American industry, suddenly in the 1930s breached corporate barriers through the massing of economic and political power and finally compelled their acceptance as bargaining representatives of employees.

The chapter began with ugly, naked power—sit-down strikes, seizure of plants, mass picketing, and all the other manifestations of industrial warfare. Management attempted first to resist and then to contain the unions. But eventually it came to terms with them and began to negotiate and administer trade-union agreements.

Perhaps the key events in the development of constitutionalism occurred in 1937 and 1948. In the former year, United States Steel, under the leadership of Myron Taylor, signed an agreement with John L. Lewis to the effect that the Steelworkers' Organizing Committee would be recognized in those plants where a majority so voted. Other steel companies did not follow the example of United States Steel. Indeed, they continued, with few exceptions, to resist unions, and one of the most violent strikes occurred in 1937—the so-called "Little Steel" strike. By 1941, however, these companies, under the pressure of the National Labor Relations Board and our increasing involvement in the war, also recognized the United Steelworkers of America and entered upon an era of negotiation and accommodation.

The war imposed a truce on industrial strife. The War Labor Board administered a form of compulsory arbitration. Strikes could legally take place, but when the Labor Board cited to the President its inability to effect a settlement in an industry considered essential for the pursuit of war, he would order it seized. Such seizures were few in number and, on the whole, corporations and unions bowed to the directives of the War Labor Board, as one would naturally expect in time of war.

When the war was over, corporation and union began to negotiate on their own, but with considerable pressure from the White House to avoid shutdowns. Nevertheless, the first postwar year recorded the greatest number of days lost through strikes in our history.

In 1948, the other critical year marking a turning point toward constitutionalism, General Motors negotiated the first of a series of long-term agreements with the United Auto Workers. That agreement established a logical framework for wage determination based upon (1) increased productivity and (2) fluctuations in living costs. Thus logical criteria—instead of crude power—projected the principle of constitutionalism to wage determination. Eventually, in one form or another, the General Motors framework became the pattern for industry.

Thus from 1948 on, it might well be said that corporate

management had decided that it would accept unions as a permanent, legitimate institution with which it would work out "rules of the game." Unions, for their part, having achieved legitimacy, gradually began to throw off the militant tactics of raw power which they had developed during their early organizing days. The 1948 agreement was renewed in 1950 for five years, and again in 1955 for three years. By that time, with necessary variations from industry to industry, it had virtually become the constitutional framework for the development of industrial relations in this country.

It should be noted that although this constitutionalism grew out of industrial warfare, the latter stages of its development were peaceful. It is to the credit of corporate management that it recognized before long that trade unions had established themselves as going institutions and accepted the challenge to integrate unions in the industrial framework of the country, while at the same time retaining the freedom and flexibility essential to conduct industry efficiently. It is well to remember that people who enjoy unilateral power do not give it up gladly. They may be willing to practice benevolence and generosity, but they resist when the things that they have been giving are demanded as rights. Industrial management is no exception to this rule. As history goes, it is to the credit of management that war over the distribution of power between corporations and unions came to an end in a relatively short period. The battle over, both of these major institutions naturally turned their attention and skill to developing an appropriate form of constitutionalism.

Constitutionalism grows out of the negotiation of trade-union agreements. These agreements are types of constitutions. Certain powers are reserved to management—in Commons's terms, the rationing and managerial powers: decisions on plant locations, the kind of product to make, the assignment of work, discipline, and in general, the authority to initiate the acts appropriate to management. *But* these powers are subject to rights granted employees and their unions. Those rights include a definition of wages and how they may be changed, hours, seniority, vacations, holidays, sick leave, pensions, safety provisions, leave of absence, and so on. A judicial machinery is also established for the disposal of grievances, up to and including referral to an outside arbitrator.

Corruption and Disillusionment

Surely what I have just described is a truly significant development. The establishment within a few decades of a new, voluntary constitutional system supplementary to our formal constitutional government must rank as a significant achievement. But already a reaction is setting in; the achievement is overlooked. The immediate cause arose from the sensational headlines which drew attention to corruption in some unions as exposed by the McClellan senatorial committee, particularly in the teamsters, the bakery workers, the AFL textile workers, the operating engineers, and several smaller unions.

To say that the community is less than happy with unions would surely be an understatement. In the 1950s labor finds itself in the doghouse—just as business occupied that unenviable spot in the 1930s. Every time a major negotiation begins, the community is perturbed by the possibility of a strike in a basic industry like steel or automobiles—with all the implications that such a stoppage has for other interrelated businesses. Again, when workers shut down the subways of New York, or immobilize tugboats and harbor shipping, an almost preceptible tremor goes through the nation. Finally, as a result of successive wage increases and fringe benefits won by unions since the war, the major problem of inflation has been laid at their door.

Indeed, it is probably more accurate to say that a considerable segment of the community—even union sympathizers—is disillusioned, if not shocked, by recent developments in unions. And this disillusionment is all the more poignant because of the way in which labor was romanticized when it was a weak, underprivileged group.

Have we made the error of expecting too much from trade unions? If so, why? And what are the implications of racketeering and corruption for the new constitutionalism? To be sure, corruption is insignificant in the total picture; only a small percentage of unions are affected by it, and the major problem lies in the strategic position which the unions collectively occupy as a major power group. But the fact that corruption is not widespread does not make it less serious. Morality is important for its own sake, and we shall have to come to grips with all the current problems that immorality has created.

Most Romantic

Of all groups, labor has probably been the most sentimentalized and romanticized. From Biblical days on, the "toiler" has been the object of special concern, charity, and compassion. With the Industrial Revolution and the growth of the factory system, human exploitation certainly flourished. Workingmen began to organize into unions, but they were suppressed; strikes were adjudged conspiratorial and illegal, and union leaders imprisoned. Even into the second decade of the twentieth century, the term sweatshop was well known.

Thus it was natural for a humane nation, heir to the Judaeo-Christian tradition and the ethical concepts of American democracy, to be moved by the plight of the man who labored, the woman who had to leave her family for ten hours a day to help make a living for her children, and the children who had to leave school to go into mines or factories to supplement family income. Indeed, the recruitment of women and children into the work force intensified the sentimentalism already attached to the working classes—to workers as workers, with an inherent nobility that would express itself if only it were not suppressed by the harsh conditions of labor.

It was the dream of idealists that the labor movement would usher in the brave new world. Thus the Labour party of Britain and the social democratic parties of much of Western Europe are an outgrowth of working-class movements influenced by socialist doctrine.

In this country, too, early labor unions played from time to time with revolutionary ideas, but not for long; in keeping with pragmatic America, unions threw off radical aspirations and addressed themselves to the practical gains they could achieve in the here and now, in the form of better wages and improved working conditions. With the triumph of the AFL over the Knights of Labor in the 1880s, the issue was settled. Under the leadership of Samuel Gompers, the most practical labor movement in the world developed.

But even in practical, nonideological America, as unions called strikes and drew attention to the unfavorable conditions under which people worked in clothing, textiles, coal, packing, steel, and on the waterfront, the rest of the community was moved by a sympathetic attitude toward labor. Industrial relations commissions were appointed to delve into the causes of unrest. A literature sprang up portraying the unhappy lot of the working classes. Prolabor sympathy found its greatest expression during the Depression of the 1930s with its massive unemployment and destitution. The Roosevelt Administration threw its weight behind the labor movement; the National Labor Relations Board so conceived and administered its mandate as virtually to help unions become firmly established in the economy of the nation —undoubtedly with the approval of the majority of the nation, judging by presidential and congressional votes, at least until the passing of the Taft-Hartley Act in 1947.

All the more because of this public, romantic support of an "underdog" group, it came as a shock to discover that these unions were not dedicated social organizations, but powerful groups exerting constant pressure on industry for increased wages and fringe benefits under enlarged social security programs. And in 1957 came the greatest disillusionment of all in revelations of corruption and racketeering, of self-aggrandizement on the part of leaders, of the emasculation of democratic processes within these unions, of the establishment of virtual dictatorships, and of the practice of resorting again and again to the Fifth Amendment when pressed for evidence by a senatorial committee.

The greater the romanticism, the more the danger of disillusionment. And disillusionment can be even more dangerous for social policy than romance. It is therefore time for sober stocktaking. Only then can we build a realistic constitutionalism as a basis for a moral framework.

Even though corruption is uncovered now and then in some sector of government, we do not turn against our constitutional system. Indeed we seek to strengthen it. Just so must we approach the necessary but difficult task of creating constitutionalism in industry.

24

Realities of Union Power

LET us first try to grasp the simple fact that we are dealing with a major sector of the American community. With eighteen million breadwinners as actual members, perhaps forty to fifty million Americans are involved directly and indirectly in unions. We must assume they constitute a normal distribution—average people, some exceptional, some mediocre; a majority of them honest, a minority dishonest.

In other words, we must accept union members as typical Americans. We should not be surprised, then, if they behave within the framework of American values and goals.

Of course, not all unions are alike any more than all corporations are alike. They differ a great deal—depending on their history, the quality of their leadership, the origin and distribution of their members, the industry in which they operate, the type of corporations they deal with, and so forth. But, allowing for differences, what are their common characteristics? Perhaps the best way to approach this question is to see what a union is not:

1. A union though perhaps idealistic in origin, is a practical, usually hard-boiled organization with its eye on securing material gains for its members and, at the same time, enhancing the prestige and power of its leaders.

2. A union is not a revolutionary organization. On the contrary, it belongs among the most conservative. Unions are in the forefront fighting communism; they are impatient even with socialism. The vast majority of leaders and members—perhaps as many as 95 per cent—vote the straight Democratic or even the Republican ticket.

3. A union is not a public-service organization. It is primarily interested in its own members and in its own leadership. Of course, like all economic and political groups, a union may well argue that to the extent it serves its members it also serves the public. Nevertheless, it is essentially a self-interest organization; its primary aim is to get the very best wages, hours, and working conditions for its members.

4. A union is not a democratic organization. Although virtually every union has a constitution, stemming from its early grass-roots character, which provides for the usual democratic procedures such as secret ballots, periodic elections of officers, and regular conventions made up of delegates from the respective locals to formulate and adopt policies, behind this democratic façade stands a political machine.

5. Trade unions are not polite or well mannered or even diplomatic in their dealings with corporation executives, or even with government officials. Indeed, they usually adopt a posture of hostility, at least publicly, as they organize pressure to attain their objectives.

Role of Power

All of these negative aspects stem from the fundamental nature of unions. A union is a power organization. Its positive role is to mobilize economic, political, and moral power to win objectives for members and leaders. To do so, it will even compete with other unions, as is evidenced by recurrent jurisdictional disputes, the most hardy perennial unsolved problem in the house of labor. Nor will any union sacrifice a possible gain so that members of another union may benefit, even though its standards may already be higher. The auto workers, or steel workers, or printers, for example, do not forego making demands for higher wages in order that the lower-paid workers in other industries may catch up to them.

But this does not mean that the unions do not serve a useful purpose. To illustrate by an admitted oversimplification of function: if corporations are placed on one side and unions on the other, the one to maximize profits, the other to maximize wages and working conditions—it may be seen at once that they complement each other. Both groups are given the right under law to withdraw from the market if they deem the price offered for their products or services inadequate, and the bargaining activity between them produces prices and wages that approximate a sort of practical justice. (Of course, the consumer also has the right to withdraw from the market if exorbitant prices reflect too large a profit or too high a wage; indeed, the consumer is the ultimate sovereign with veto power in a three-cornered bargaining process.)

Hence our disillusionment with unions for failure to fulfill our romantic vision of idealism and public service should not mislead us into thinking we can dispense with them. Without the pressure of unions, wages and working conditions would be depressed to subnormal levels. Sweatshops did not come into being because employers of their day were evil, but because, in the absence of unions, there was no counterpressure to keep wages up to certain levels, which all competitors had to meet if they were to attract and hold labor. And sweatshops could happen again, under the pressure of competition, even though the overwhelming sentiment of the community would be against them.

It is for this reason that both the Taft-Hartley Act and the Wagner Act, though differing fundamentally in their posture toward organized labor, gave as their objective, in their respective preambles, the establishment of equality of bargaining power as desirable from the viewpoint of the public welfare and made mandatory the recognition of unions as bargaining representatives if a majority of employees so vote.

As Marketing Agency

It is from the perspective of a power system that one can best understand the nature and function of trade unions. First and primarily, a union is a combination of a political and business organization. From the business point of view a union is primarily a marketing agency. Every union is essentially a collectivity for selling labor as a unit in the form of various skills. All its other activities are directed to making this selling function as effective as possible.

To be sure, unions do not think of themselves primarily as marketing agencies; they still harbor in their own minds the image derived from their origin, namely a social movement launched to wrest a fair break for themselves from reluctant owners. Although hardly a union president subscribes to the concept of a class struggle or the nationalization of the tools of production and distribution, nevertheless labor representatives talk as if they were in a permanent contest with capitalist employers. Such sentiments are invoked in union convention sessions, during union election campaigns, and during preparations for and actual negotiation with corporations.

If, however, we keep in mind the function of a union as a marketing agency, we see that what looks like political propaganda is in reality part of a merchandising campaign particularly suited to its purpose of exacting the price desired as wages for its membership. Thus, union leaders and the whole union apparatus drum up emotionalism, ring the changes on the injustice of Wall Street and the justice of their cause, hold special conventions, go on radio and television, threaten strikes, all to dramatize their cause. And since the strike is raw power, its potential use has to be justified in political and moral phraseology

—the workers against capital. In other words, it has to be sold to the membership, so that they will be willing to undergo the sacrifices entailed, and to the community, so that it will be willing to suffer the inconveniences consequent on a strike.

Thus every major negotiation is launched by a large-scale promotional campaign in which union demands are projected in terms of a moral cause calling for a living wage; advancing standards of living; security against hazards of unemployment, sickness, and old age; and, in recent years, purchasing power necessary to keep the wheels of industry moving.

It may well be that if all this militant union activity during negotiations were understood as a sales promotion campaign with a political flavor, it would upset us less. We do not get upset when corporations or political parties put on their campaigns. We read or ignore the advertisements; we look at, or turn off, television plays and radio skits. On the whole, we maintain a skeptical attitude.

Of course, the possibility of a strike makes the union campaign more of a threat than either the usual sales or political campaigns. Strikes spell loss not only to employees but also to merchants, landlords, and all the other people dependent on the continuous functioning of the business. But strikes are legal in a democracy, and every once in a while we have to undergo the discomforts attending a shutdown. Indeed, if we learned to take a calmer, more naturalistic attitude toward strikes, unions might be more sober and restrained in using them. It is the threat of their use that causes fear and capitulation, even when management may be convinced that it is wiser to face a shutdown than to grant the price demanded by the unions and the workers.

Centralized Power

The trade union, then, is a power organization putting pressure on management for advancing wages and working conditions. From its nature as a power center stems the necessity for centralized administration. Since in the final analysis the threat of shutdown determines the price which a corporation will pay for labor, a union must be able to initiate and conduct strikes, and a well-organized strike is essentially an exercise in military strategy and tactics calling for highly centralized decision making. It is a form of blockade. Hence the weapons that trouble businessmen and the community in general come into play—the picket line and the boycott. But once we grant the legitimacy of a strike as a weapon in the negotiating process, then we must also grant the legitimacy of using the weapons which make the strike effective.

The tendency toward centralization in American trade unions is therefore rooted in their militant origin. From the beginnings until well into the 1930s, only by means of a military strategy could the unions make any progress and hold on to any gains they might have made from time to time. Such strategy called for planning from the top—for deploying organizers, throwing up picket lines, establishing commissaries, providing legal assistance, and raising money to finance this widespread military activity. Unions had to "crash the gate," to force their way into industry. Such was the case with the old AFL unions, as with the younger CIO unions. The major difference was that, by the time the CIO got going, trade unionism and collective bargaining enjoyed legal backing.

It was his qualities as a military strategist that made John L. Lewis the natural leader of the CIO in its early days. By temperament he enjoyed the posture of a fighter, and by experience in the coal fields he had become adept at applying military tactics to enlisting union recruits in a hostile environment. He also had available funds from the miners' treasury to defray the costs incurred in the early stages of organizing workmen in the mass-production industries. Of all the major steel companies, for instance, only United States Steel forestalled recourse to violent tactics; and that was in the form of a secret compact—one more instance of top-level strategy—the Taylor-Lewis understanding, which in 1937 granted, as already indicated, the Steelworkers' Organizing Committee bargaining rights in any plant where the majority of employees so voted.

Lewis brought with him from the coal miners' union a team experienced in this type of militant organizing—men like Philip Murray, Van A. Bittner, and Allen S. Haywood. Thus, even though a large segment of local workers in the centers of heavy industry may have been discontented and desirous of union organization, it was old, seasoned leaders from the miners, to whom were added veterans like Sidney Hillman, David Dubinsky, and Emil Rieve from the needle trades and textiles, who took over and directed the campaigns. Thus, the very militaristic origin of trade unionism propelled unions into a centralized form of government.

Logic of Negotiation

Then, after the union is already recognized and doing business with corporations, the very logic of negotiations strengthens the tendency toward centralization. As demands by the membership for wage increases and economic gains are repeated at each contract negotiation, they lose some of their value and potency. The farsighted leader has to conceive of new demands which he can justify.

For instance, Philip Murray launched the demand for pensions in 1949 and led his men into a strike to secure noncontributory pensions. It was an open secret that the rank and file entertained little enthusiasm for the strike, and Murray had personally to visit steel communities to maintain their morale. The men walked out in loyalty to him, but, as typical Americans, they would rather have had a larger pay envelope immediately then enjoy a pension in the dim future. Similarly, in 1955, Walter P. Reuther projected a plan for guaranteed annual wages or what in reality became supplementary unemployment benefits.

Here, incidentally, is a desirable function of leadership—to be able to shift strategy with changing conditions and, above all, to look ahead and provide for future contingencies. *Vox populi* may be *vox Dei,* but it is often fixed on immediate, earthy desires. The leader must think of the morrow.

Finally, the actual requirements of negotiations when the adversaries meet around the table call for centralized decision making. Under the conditions of present-day America, a strike is questionable because unions have achieved status and influence. Wages are already at a high level. A strike spells hardship and debt to the workers; also lost business to the employer and to all those in the community dependent indirectly upon the enterprise. Therefore, the union leader engaged in negotiating must, as the zero hour approaches, decide whether to put a strike into effect or to make compromises—as offers and counteroffers are being placed on the table. Indeed, at this final stage, negotiators are usually reduced in number to a few on each side to expedite matters without too many debates by the crowd. It is not feasible under these circumstances to go back to the ranks for a plebiscite. Commitments must be made, and with a fairly good degree of assurance that they are enforceable.

Again, after the settlement has been made and the agreement signed, the union official must be sure that the members will live up to it in the various plants of the corporation. There is always the danger of "dragging feet" or even of walkouts. Hence, the leader must have a bureaucracy ready to go out into the field and obtain ratification of the agreement; and, if ranks break away and engage in strikes, he must be certain of a strong enough following to feel confident that before long the men will be brought to their senses and return to their workbenches. The commitment made to management must be carried out if he is to enjoy confidence at the next negotiation.

Authoritarian Nature

These factors, among others, make the government of unions characteristically authoritarian. The president is the "boss." The constitution provides for an executive council, but a majority of those on it are usually his men. Conventions are held and the delegates are elected by local unions, but he usually appoints the international representatives and organizers, who are the ones that get out the votes for the administration, whenever necessary. Essentially, it is a leadership function which the president discharges, and therefore he must be sure he has a loyal group that will go along with him.

It is also in the interest of the corporation that the union leadership be centralized and authoritarian. The keeping of commitments at the work level is a matter of life and death to management. It must price its commodity and be able to make deliveries. If the successive steps in reaching compromises had to go back to the union hall for debate and ratification, one would run the inevitable risk inherent in political hustings—the delays and interruptions that arise from political oppositions and factions.

Indeed, the intrinsic logic both of union administration and of corporate economics makes the practice of grass-roots democracy within unions almost impossible. Once the management of a corporation and union officials begin to appreciate each other's needs in this respect, there arises some understanding of the range of bargaining limits in a practical world, even though the astute union official will always try to stretch the limit to the utmost, whereas the prudent company executive will try to stay well within the limits of adding to his costs.

Thus, we find that, although union officials and corporate managements start from opposite sides of the pole—one elected, the other appointed—they end up pretty much at the same point: both are highly centralized, authoritarian governors of power systems. One vital difference does remain; management need not face political campaigns for reelection. Union presidents start out as elected officials; reelection is required under the constitution. Nevertheless, they are reelected again and again until death or voluntary retirement. And often the trade-union president, like the corporation president, may have a decisive voice in his succession.

In what we might call personality structures, too, union and corporate presidents have a striking resemblance. They are both strong men, enjoy power, and do not suffer dissidents gladly. Thus John L. Lewis—an extreme example of the autocrat—had his erstwhile and lifelong comrades, William Green and Philip Murray, expelled from the United Mine Workers when their paths parted on his withdrawal from both the AFL and CIO. He did not retire to his own tent to sulk, though, but issued fulminations against all and sundry (including President Roosevelt) who would not go along with him.

In this one respect, indeed, the union president still resembles the former owner-president more than the modern professional administrator. It is *his* union, he bled and fought for it, just as the rugged individualist of a generation ago brooked no interference in his business which he had fought and bled for. John L. Lewis, George Meany, Walter P. Reuther, and David Dubinsky, though differing in so many ways, have in common the quality of making themselves felt whenever they enter any conference, be it in an executive suite or hotel negotiating room, in the White House or Madison Square Garden.

The moral is clear: such men accentuate the centralizing drift that is inherent in the institutions they lead.

Indifferent Members

It is doubtful whether union members are much concerned about the course democracy has taken in their unions or feel seriously deprived because they do not participate actively in the government of their organizations.

For one thing, unlike earlier generations, current members do not have the fervor or excitement of founders. The pioneers were workers at the bench who, smarting under harsh conditions and an oppressive atmosphere, faced personal risks when they rallied to the call for organization as a way of obtaining a voice in their industrial destiny. They were discharged and blacklisted or, if kept, faced constant discrimination. In one way or another, they were punished for their audacity in attempting to form unions. Strikes were long and bitter; physical violence and imprisonment were not unknown consequences. Thus, out of risks and self-sacrifice, a spirit of dedication arose.

At least until World War II, large numbers of workers participated in the struggle—breaking through the historical resistance of heavy industry to trade unionism.

With the advent of the war, however, several million members were added to union ranks largely through decisions of the War Labor Board granting unions "maintenance of membership" as a way of avoiding strikes under the necessity of uninterrupted war production. Usually the checkoff was also part of the agreement. Millions of workers were enrolled, not only new to unionism, but even—particularly in the case of many recruits from the South—new to modern industry. And since the war, the four million new members in industry know even less of the sacrifices their predecessors underwent so that they could now enjoy the best working conditions and the highest wages in the world.

As corporation after corporation, under the constant pressure of governmental and union power, yielded recognition and bargaining rights and negotiated contracts from year to year, the rank and file became more and more apathetic. This is not to say that today's workers do not know what they want. On the contrary, they look on unions as a vehicle primarily for getting them higher wages, along with more and better fringe benefits and sundry improvements in working conditions. Having made no real sacrifice to bring their unions into existence, they regard the dues which they pay as tantamount to buying an insurance policy guaranteeing them more and more of the good things of life. Remember that most of these members have never had to suffer the adversities of depression and prolonged unemployment; they know nothing but sustained prosperity and constantly rising wages. These new workers have also, on the whole, been spared the privations of prolonged strikes which their forefathers conducted—and generally lost because employers could keep open and hire new workers in a surplus labor market.

Today, strikes are both effective and less costly in human suffering. There is no surplus labor for employers to recruit, and workers usually have wives or younger members of the family contributing to the total family income. Under these conditions, unions have been able to break through to new levels in industries like automobiles, steel, rubber, and electrical manufacturing, which have been profitable and hence in a position to pay high wages. Thus, General Motors, Ford, and United States Steel have been pacemakers in setting high standards of compensation and fringe benefits—*after* tough bargaining with the United Auto Workers and the United Steelworkers. In other words, trade unions have been of material benefit to workers.

Pressure for Gain

Yet workers are dissatisfied. Since wage increases and other benefits have been passed on in prices, they feel that they are always chasing a rising cost of living—higher rent, higher grocery bills, higher clothing costs. All of which highlights the constant pressure exerted upon trade-union officials in serving their members as salesmen, in forever seeking more and more benefits from year to year, from contract to contract.

These new union members are bent on continuing to enjoy the good things of life and having their aspirations for a rising standard fulfilled. They respond to the constant stimulus of advertising and sales promotion. They are good customers for cars, television sets, homes, furniture, travel, and vacations. They would also like to see their children enjoy the benefits of higher education. They do not hesitate to take advantage of credit facilities, even though it means going into debt. Thus, all the inner logic of the modern American trade unions is to propel trade-union leaders to ask for more material gains every time they enter into collective bargaining.

Herein lies the fallacy of attributing inflationary pressures primarily to labor leaders and to trade unions as organizations. To the extent that the wage push is a factor in the complex economics of inflation, the pressure—and it really is pressure with a full head of steam—is from union members as individual workers. The very role of union leaders as politicians makes response to these pressures inevitable. Like all politicians, even though they may build good and sturdy machines, they have to keep their ears to the ground. No politician, no matter how powerful his machine, can long survive unless he articulates the basic sentiments and desires of his electorate.

It should not be overlooked, however, that trade-union leaders are wedded to the Keynesian doctrine that the prosperity of the country is determined by the propensity to consume. No matter how conservative, they hold to the doctrine that high purchasing power is the key to prosperity. Accordingly, they take the position that the constant demand for higher wages and better working conditions not only is justified for workers but is good for the whole country.

Democracy Reconsidered

I trust that what I have depicted as developments in unions will not disillusion the reader about democracy or in any way give the impression that I am cynical about its actual and potential worth. The lesson to learn is that pure democracy is not always appropriate to all social and economic institutions. We ourselves, after the founding of the nation, had to rely on political parties to make our Constitution work in a practical, rivalrous, and competitive world. Thus, unions, having to meet the exigencies first of fighting and then of negotiating and making commitments, had no alternative but to devise a form of government that would centralize strategy, tactics, and decision making.

Nor should it be overlooked that, in a very real sense, the concept of a union as a democratic organization continues to be important. For the machinery by which those in power can be ousted is present. And arguments in dissent do take place on union convention floors.

As long as such opportunity for dissent remains, then somehow democracy continues as a vital faith. The tragedy revealed by the McClellan committee lies in the fact that in some unions —by connivance and corrupt alliances with racketeers like Dio —terrorism, violence, and murder have been introduced to stifle any opposition, and democracy has been subverted and turned into a shambles.

Perhaps it is just as well, as we scrutinize the workings of democracy in government, business, unions, or whatever the institution, to admit that in its pure sense democracy, like morality, is an aspiration rather than a living, everyday reality. Since the days of New England town government with its town meeting, we have had precious little pure democracy. Size, scale, bigness—call it what you will—added to the increasingly technical complexity of problems and their solutions has made us all leave these matters more and more to professionals and the technicians. In this regard the shape of things as they are emerging in the union world confirms the trend.

25

Constitutional Government and the Loyal Opposition

On the whole, the typical union president and his colleagues are conservative. In Europe—England, for instance—they would be considered Tories in their political thinking. In America, we would probably place them somewhat left of center in our political spectrum.

With but few exceptions, the American labor leader is a New Dealer. He is a Roosevelt and Truman partisan. He believes in and works for the welfare state, not because of a predilection for the theory underlying it, but as a way of assuring support for collective bargaining and for adequate legislative programs to meet basic hazards—unemployment, sickness, substandard wages, industrial accidents, and so forth. In particular, he is bent on employing the full power of government to prevent unemployment, the one hazard that shadows American workers more than any other. If, in spite of all attempts, recession sets in, he will insist that government on all levels help create jobs, whether directly by public works or indirectly by stimulating demand for the products of private industry.

The typical American labor leader believes in private enterprise. Not only is he militantly anticommunist and impatient even with the mild socialism of the British or Scandinavian variety, but he is proud of the productive record of American industry. Indeed, he acts as an enthusiastic spokesman for American capitalism when abroad, which is quite often these days, as a delegate at international conferences.

Aggressive Bargaining

One characteristic the labor leader must have: he must be an effective representative of his members in obtaining high wages and good conditions for them; and these must be on the constant rise. He is impatient with the reluctance of business executives to grant these demands, though he himself realizes that even in prosperous America ceilings exist on what can be obtained at any one negotiation. In this respect he is more seasoned than his membership, who understand little of business economics and are impatient to fulfill as rapidly as possible the dream of the rising American standard of living.

The labor leader looks on today's business executives, not as chief owners, but as hired men just like the production workers whom he represents. He does not mind twitting these executives about the high salaries and the other emoluments they have been able to negotiate for themselves during the last quarter-century while being shocked when the same things in principle are requested for their employees.

The typical union president enjoys negotiations and the headlines that go with it. If at times he struts the stage quoting Shakespeare and the Bible—well, that is his way of putting on a show as a merchandiser. He usually assumes a political posture in which the corporation is portrayed as the "unreasonable" and "ungenerous" opposition. He represents the "people"; his opponent in business protects "property" rights. He is adept in the use of the strike weapon as a threat and tactical weapon to put management on the defensive. At the same time, he respects astute bargaining by his corporate opposition. He is also adept in arriving at a compromise settlement and in maneuvering his membership into accepting it.

When it comes to internal union administration, however, the typical union president does not make a good showing. He has grown up in a fighting atmosphere and is slow to see the necessity of setting up an appropriate organization for day-to-day administration. The whole problem of training, decentralization, and long-range planning cries out for attention.

To be sure, the present size and growth of trade unions is a relatively recent matter. Fifty years ago, corporations were also slow in realizing the importance of setting up an adequate administrative organization to carry forward their programs; indeed, the widespread growth of education for business administrators is a matter of the last few decades. Hopefully, trade unions will also develop educational programs in cooperation with universities. As of now, with but few exceptions, they still do not see the need. Their educational programs are elementary and cast largely in the old indoctrination atmosphere of the days of struggle. They have, however, added *technical* staffs of economists, statisticians, publicists, and specialists in insurance programs. These new staffs, incidentally, have accentuated the trend toward centralization, since by necessity they work closely with top leaders, usually the president, rather than with the rank and file.

At the local level, union administration is even in a much poorer state than at headquarters. Staffs are inadequate and untrained. On the whole, very little is done to acquaint the members with the content of a union contract and to guide them from day to day. Indeed, once an agreement has been signed, things are left to a sort of "let nature take its course" policy. It is well for management to beware of this. It must take on the task of administering the agreement and expect little more from the union than serving as a policeman or a watchdog to see that members' rights are not violated.

In many respects the union president is coming more and

more to resemble the modern-day professional manager as contrasted with the former owner-manager. He dresses well. His salary is rising; in most cases it is nothing like that of a corporation president, yet 50,000 dollars a year is not unknown. He does not enjoy perquisites like stock options and bonuses; on the other hand, liberal expense accounts are common. The trade-union leader lives rather well when away from home, which is a great deal of the time. He puts up at the best hotels. On the whole the union is anxious to make things comfortable and perhaps even plushy for its executive, but an element of pride also enters. The union feels that its president should meet his opposite number from the corporation on an equal basis.

In his own community, too, the typical union president is active, just like business executives, in community funds and in cultural and civic activities.

Government and Opposition

There is little danger that the unions will try to invade seriously the realm of managerial functions. By and large, union presidents realize they do not have the technical knowledge about production, marketing, finance, and all the other major functions that enter into the running of a modern corporation. They actually prefer to remain in the opposition—where they are in a better position to talk from time to time about "capacity to pay," demand to "see the books," ask to share in bonuses, or criticize management for inefficiency.

All in all, we might say that a relationship is developing which projects management as "the government of the day" and unions as "the permanent opposition"—increasingly becoming a "loyal opposition" in the political sense. That is to say, it is an opposition that puts constant pressure on "the government" to improve the substance of the union contract every time it expires; between negotiations, it serves as a policing agency in the enforcement of the contract. Beyond the corporation, the "opposition" raises questions about unemployment, recessions, purchasing power, and government action to advance the welfare of the people.

All this is part of the development mentioned earlier—the emergence of a private, or voluntary, constitutional framework for our economic life which is complementary to the formal constitutional framework of our political life. In this voluntary constitutional government, business management is in charge of organizing and managing corporate activities to turn out goods and services for the community. It thus becomes the initiating government. The union is the opposition which raises questions and challenges managerial action—all to the end of seeing that labor obtains as large a share as possible of the wealth created. (And, again, the community has a final veto by refusing to buy if the price becomes exorbitant.)

This constitutional system is established and maintained through the activity of negotiation and bargaining. When a contract expires, what amounts to a political campaign takes place in the preparation and actual negotiation of the new contract. A strike may take place, but such strikes are becoming less frequent and, when they do occur, more and more friendly, reflecting the disagreement of parties as to the terms on which they can continue as government and opposition. It is not likely that we will again witness, except sporadically as in the Kohler episode, the violence and the deep hatred which accompanied strikes during the nineteenth century and the early years of this century when unions were battling for recognition and a constitutional system had not yet been born.

Arbitration as Final Court

One of the most dramatic developments in this new constitutional system is the almost universal provision for arbitration by disinterested outsiders in the event of disagreement—

something that would have been thought improbable when the surge of unionism got under way in the 1930s.

The American Arbitration Association and the Federal Mediation Service keep panels of names from which parties themselves choose an arbitrator for a particular dispute; the larger companies and unions have established full-time year-round arbitration offices of their own. These arbitrators are recruited typically from university faculties, particularly from economics departments, law schools, and business schools. They are well remunerated—not quite up to the standard of company executives, but not far from those of union leaders. Their decisions are now reported by several services, just like appellate court decisions, with a volume published each year.

Indeed, arbitration is a court—the court of last resort after the grievance machinery is invoked. Awards and decisions are binding. And although precedents do not have the same weight in industrial arbitration that they have in courts of law, nevertheless they are not without their influence in building up guides for decision and action. The arbitrators have now established an academy to mark their arrival as professionals; they hold annual meetings to discuss common problems, formulate ethical codes, study legislative proposals, and do all the other things befitting a dignified calling.

Management's Contribution

This development of constitutionalism stands out as a major achievement in American industrial society. It has no counterpart in Europe. What looked like irreconcilable conflict in the 1930s has given way to an orderly, civilized way of adjusting differences. Legitimate power of self-made law has been substituted for illegitimate power of violence, or for law imposed by government.

Management has played no minor role in this contribution.

Corporation executives have acquired a new skill as negotiators, so much so as to be able to take in stride the power of an explosive labor movement and turn it into a productive force in the American economy. If we are inclined at times to be critical of the way wages and fringe benefits have been passed on into prices, let us remember that this has been a period of prosperity with the prospects for profits so good that prudent management would have great difficulty in justifying strikes. Moreover, corporations have faced the challenge of integrating these new and large-scale unions within the framework of American industry. Strikes would hardly have been helpful in winning the confidence of new leaders and new workers.

Indeed, at one time it was thought that such huge power centers as General Motors and the United Auto Workers would almost inevitably resort to conflict and strikes whenever they confronted each other in negotiation. Fortunately the story has turned out differently. It is not all a matter of luck; imaginativeness and creativeness on the part of corporate management have given birth to plans by means of which the successive demands of unions could be put into some logical, orderly framework—related, in particular, to the cost of living and increasing productivity.

Management representatives have also given a good account of themselves in turning arbitration into a successful judicial process. When I first started as an arbitrator a quarter of a century ago, the typical company presentation was pitiable compared with that of union officials. That is no longer true. If anything, the picture is now reversed. On the whole, corporate representatives do a much more professional job than their opposite numbers from the unions. The record speaks for itself; a vast majority of decisions, perhaps three-fourths, are found in favor of management.

Of course, a substantial number of cases appealed to arbitration by unions are "political." It is easier to have an arbitrator turn down the aggrieved ranks than for a union official to say *no.* All of this is quite consistent with the political nature of unions. (Incidentally, this has its encouraging aspect. For it shows that, even with a strong machine or bureaucracy, limits exist to the degree to which union officials can impose their judgment, even when right.) And so a goodly number of cases get lost by unions because of lack of merit. The fact remains that the dignity and the competence with which management handles its side of controversies have strengthened the forces of constitutionalism.

In so doing, American management has made a notable contribution to the resolution of conflict by the substitution of reason for emotionalism and violence.

Production and Distribution

It is all to the good that management has become by sheer logic of events the "government of the day"; for, in truth, the very nature of its function makes it the dynamic agency with major responsibility for the production of wealth. It mobilizes capital, builds factories, assembles machinery, engages labor, and establishes marketing and distribution channels. The test of profitability operating in a competitive market puts the burden of efficiency on the managerial apparatus—to produce wealth, that is, goods and services, at the lowest possible cost.

I do not mean to imply for one moment that employees and their unions are not factors in creating wealth. In fact, without them the wheels of industry would stall. But they play their part as they fit into the productive scheme projected by management. The union's primary function then becomes the equitable *distribution* of the wealth created in terms of wages, fringe benefits, and conditions of work.

A moment's reflection will show that such a distribution of function is consistent with the organization and the specialization characteristic of our American society. Management is judged by the professional criteria of good performance in turning out products and services at a price which the consumer will pay. The labor leader is judged by the effectiveness with which he advances the welfare of his members. Since management has to be productive, competitive, and profitable, limits are set as to what the labor leader and his members may obtain. In this sense, management again, by the very nature of its function, indirectly represents the other groups in the community—stockholders and consumers in particular.

Thus this voluntary constitutional system becomes a combined operation of management and union officials to keep the productive mechanism at the highest possible efficiency and with a maximum degree of practical justice for the largest number of people. In addition, the constitutional system protects employees from possible abuse as a result of management's preoccupation with efficiency. For union leaders not only market labor at the best possible bargain in terms of wages and working conditions, but they also see to it that civil rights as spelled out in the agreement are observed in the shop. In this sense, the grievance and arbitration machinery operates as a protective device to ensure that workers are not subject to capricious and intolerable treatment as their skills are mobilized in the drive for production.

In sum, as I see it, trade unions started with a great burst of raw power in the 1930s but by now have largely settled down into a combined political and business institution, marketing labor at the highest possible price and leaving it to management to be the administrators of industry. To be sure, from time to time in any particular negotiation, demands may be made which might seem to indicate that the union leadership may be invading managerial functions. Usually, however, this proves a temporary strategy. It can fairly be assumed by this time that the trade unions are content to serve as the challengers within a constitutional system in which management enjoys the responsibility of conducting the corporate enterprise.

This does not mean that major negotiations between large corporations and large unions—Ford or General Motors and the

United Automobile Workers, for instance—will not be noisy, rough, with a strike seemingly around the corner. For negotiations of this magnitude set standards and patterns for the rest of the economy and so provide a forum for fighting out fundamental issues regarding the distribution of power and wealth. But however vital and complex the issues—and this is the point—the developing constitutional framework serves to reduce the potential danger of resorting to raw power. The noise one hears from time to time is not that of mass picketing as in the 1930s, but that of "rafters ringing" in mass meetings, in special conventions, at senatorial hearings, in newspaper headlines, on radio and television.

If by chance a strike does occur, it is likely that picket lines will be token in nature only, with the few assigned at this or that gate even enjoying coffee and doughnuts sent out by an industrial relations executive from the company cafeteria. Moreover, should a crucial baseball series happen to be played, one should not be surprised if some benevolent "autocrat" sitting in his executive suite sends out word to have a loud-speaker strung up. For intuitively he senses that a home run at the crucial moment, or the suspense of a possible no-hit-no-run game as the last half of the ninth inning approaches, may well serve in this instance as a "moral equivalent for war."

Nor am I suggesting here a scenario for a movie. It already has happened. In the 1949 steel strike, doughnuts and coffee, as well as loud-speakers to broadcast the world series, were supplied by management—in a company that had been deeply involved in the violent "Little Steel" strike of the 1930s, with "no holds barred" by either side.

In brief, constitutionalism is the time-honored way in the evolution of government by which raw power has been tamed and replaced by systems of jurisprudence. And that, as I read the record, is precisely what has been happening in American industry as it has adapted itself to the thrust of newly gained power by massive trade unionism.

Inflation Reconsidered

The one major economic problem which has bedeviled us since the war—inflation—must be reconsidered in the light of its full social context. How can blame be laid at the doors of unions when they have been mainly the reflectors, rather than the initiators, of pressures by an ambitious and well-living American working population at the time of great boom prosperity? Should we expect a red-blooded American, be he an executive or machine operator, to be content with an increase of 2 or 3 per cent per year in his income just because that happens to be the average rate by which man-hour productivity rises per year?

Inflation is much more complex a matter than the simple relation of wages to prices—as has been so publicized during these last years. Can it be that a slow rise in the price level is a premium we all have to pay to operate a prosperous, dynamic economy—at least for the time being, until we learn how to maintain stable prices under prosperous conditions?

All the theories so far put forth about inflation or deflation —thoughtful and logical as they are—just do not make sense in terms of what takes place in actual life.

A new theory has to be formulated to fit the changes in our social structure which have come to a head since the 1930s. In earlier days, wage earners and farmers paid the major price for the instability—with its accompanying fluctuations in employment and prices—that characterized our economy. Today, through legislation, political pressure, and collective bargaining, wage earners and farmers are protected against a fall in their income when working and against destitution when unemployed. It is savers and fixed-income receivers who have no such bargaining power, that now bear the cost—not in terms of unemployment, but rather in the shrinking value of their dollars. Their bargaining power is further diminished by the fact that industry no longer depends on them for capital, but gets a large part of the money needed for retooling and expansion either from earnings or from collective funds held by foundations, pension and welfare funds, and investment trusts.

In the 1920s—also a period of prosperity—holders of fixed incomes and investors did relatively well (until the speculative orgy overtook them), though large groups of the population were actually depressed—particularly the farmers, coal miners, and textile workers. How unstable the whole structure actually was came home dramatically in 1929.

With the Roosevelt regime came a more active program on the part of the Federal government in which wage earners, farmers, and small debtors became the primary concern—to the disadvantage of investors and those who lived on fixed incomes. This shift has never been reversed. Meanwhile, businessmen have learned how to turn the new situation into a vast market for consumer goods. The defense needs of the nation have added to both the demand for workers and the amount of income to be spent. Full employment is now the goal of every administration, Republican or Democratic. Perhaps what we need now is a new economic theory of depression and prosperity to supplement that of Keynes which was addressed to the Great Depression and how to emerge from it.

Meanwhile, until that comes about, perhaps we should make up our minds that there may be worse problems than the moderate inflation we have been experiencing—unemployment for one, and social unrest for another.

26

Abuse and Needed Legislation

EVEN as we hail the development of constitutionalism between unions and corporations, we must not fail to address ourselves to the critical question as to what to do about the excesses which have developed in a minority of unions—corruption, infiltration by racketeers, abuse of office, and collusive arrangements at the expense both of workers and the community. Indeed, in industry as in government, liberty and due process under law thrive only in an atmosphere of eternal vigilance. For pathological dangers are always in the making. They stem from the basic age-old problem of power and its tendency to corrupt and destroy unless checked and directed into constructive, moral directions.

Looked at realistically, it is a tribute to the inherent decency of Americans that the sudden acquisition of great power by unions and labor leaders has not wreaked damage on a much larger sector of labor and industry. It is a matter of good fortune that the malpractices of the teamsters' leadership have not overtaken other unions, particularly those that have jurisdiction in the heartland of industry—in steel, automobiles, rubber, airplanes, machine tools, electrical manufacturing, and so forth.

Fortunately, also, the leaders of the newly merged AFL-CIO are not only deeply perturbed but have actually placed highest on their agenda the cleaning out of corrupt elements. George

Meany and his associates have literally taken their coats off and gone to work so vigorously that some fear that they run the risk of precipitating internecine warfare among unions, with the teamsters and all their power for potential troublemaking in the vanguard.

Under Meany's leadership, codes of ethical practices have already been developed and procedures set up for charges, hearings, and appropriate disciplinary action. This program is actively in operation; a number of unions have already been expelled and others given notice to clean house or face expulsion. It is safe to predict that, by and large, the action taken thus far will no doubt have a restraining and cleansing influence in the union world.

Major Objectives

Nevertheless, the time has come for legislation. For it is doubtful whether the AFL-CIO can do the job by itself. Legislation should, however, be such as to facilitate the procedures already launched by the central federation. In the final analysis no outside agency or inspector can detect corruption as well as insiders who are dedicated to seeing to it that the moral purposes of their organizations are not subverted.

The legislative program should have four major objectives:

1. To ensure that the vast funds accumulating in union treasuries and in pension and welfare funds are as scrupulously invested and safeguarded as are any insurance or banking funds.

2. To help unions maintain their democratic framework. Adequate checks should be set up—not against the drift toward centralization, for that is inevitable, but against the danger of oppressiveness and denial of civil rights of members. With union security clauses so widespread, the opportunity to work depends a great deal on how a man stands in his union. Unions might well consider introducing the machinery established some time ago by the Upholsterers' Union, and more recently by the United

Auto Workers—an arbitration panel made up of outside public representatives to which any member may appeal if he feels he has been wronged.

But we should not leave so important a matter to the slow action of union presidents. Some watchdog agency should be set up in the Federal government, just as other agencies have been set up to scrutinize corporate behavior. A step in the right direction is the proposal of Secretary of Labor James P. Mitchell for the creation of a commissioner in the Department of Labor with power to subpoena, to receive reports, and to hold hearings as to whether provisions for elections and reports to members are observed.

3. To safeguard workers and the community against unfair practices by unions. A fresh study should be made of picketing to compel an employer to accept a union, though the employees themselves have indicated no sure desire. Similarly, secondary boycotts need a fresh examination to protect the interests of enterprises not directly involved in a labor dispute.

4. To appoint periodically a legislative committee similar to the current one headed by Senator McClellan to throw the searchlight of public attention on union practices. Perhaps even more than legislation, such hearings may, in the end, be of greatest help to Meany and his associates in the difficult task of keeping unscrupulous men from exploiting American workers and the community for their self-aggrandizement.

Men who are given large grants of power should be under constant scrutiny to give an accounting of themselves far beyond the technical requirements of the law. This is the sort of function admirably served by congressional committees in this country as by royal commissions in Britain, though one could wish that our committees modeled themselves on the judicial procedures of the British royal commissions instead of relying as much as they do on a prosecuting technique to uncover sensational behavior.

In summary, the American labor movement arose out of urgent human needs. Although it is futile to expect a revival of the moral fervor that accompanied its early years, an important and necessary task still remains for unions. They provide a way of keeping a humane balance in the rough-and-tumble of competitive economic life. Moreover, the establishment of industrial constitutionalism has resulted in a measure of justice for workers such as was unknown prior to the advent of unions.

Further, whereas many former sympathizers may be disillusioned with the way these unions have developed, such disillusionment is due more to past overromanticization of expectations than to the sober reality of what has actually happened. For, instead of bringing in a utopian brave new world, unions have taken a practical turn in obtaining substantial benefits for their members, reducing the incidence of raw power in their dealings with management, and developing, together with corporations, a supplementary constitutional system which provides a maximum degree of accommodation between management, as the government of the day, and unions, as the opposition. In all of this, management has played a major role.

As for corruption, it is up to thoughtful people in business and in the community to create a helpful atmosphere, not by punitive legislation against all unions, but specifically against those guilty of wrongdoing, and by rallying as friends rather than as enemies of the new leaders in the AFL-CIO who, for the first time, have shown courage in coming to grips with the sinister influences in their ranks.

In this way, we may make our best contribution to the age-old problem of facing up to the economic and political power which, in the form of the modern labor movement, is bound to remain with us into the indefinite future, and of keeping it headed toward moral goals and away from corruption.

For, basically, the labor movement has resulted in achieving justice and equity for the wage earners of the nation—both in the form of substantial material gains and in the freedom and status that go with citizenship, a condition that previously prevailed only in the political realm.

27

Corporate Constitutionalism: An Open Experiment

REFLECTION on the experience of corporate management with trade unions is a sobering experience. It shows up the grim realities inherent in the adventure of establishing justice through constitutionalism. Old abuses may be corrected but new ones creep in. Thus the development of constitutionalism remains always unfinished business.

Moreover, even after a relationship has been worked out between a corporation and a union, and a fairly strong constitutional system established, the going is still rough. Differences arise daily as to how a contract clause should be interpreted in a particular case of seniority, wage adjustment, or discipline. Much greater strain arises when a contract expires and a new one is to be negotiated. Who is to say, for instance, what wage or what production standard is just and right? Certain criteria are available but they are not indisputable either scientifically or morally.

Differences are sharp on issues of this sort. The "right" price or workload is reached only when the parties agree upon it. And agreement is reached because, in addition to logic and appeal to the decent opinion of the community, raw power in the form of a strike or lockout is always in the background as a final arbiter. The parties weigh the costs of a possible resort to industrial warfare—costs in money, in health, in morale, in good will. Hence, when the parties agree to the terms of their new contract—that is to say, their constitution—they declare that they have in fact reached fair and just decisions, in a workable sense, on wages, productivity, and all the other elements that enter into their working relationship. They agree that in so far as they are concerned, this is for the time being the best balance they can agree upon for doing justice to all parties. They prefer their bargains and compromises to a resort to raw power.

Again, as is true with the negotiating process at the bargaining table, so with the judicial procedure as embodied in the grievance machinery. It does not always present a polite, well-ordered, pretty affair. The judges do not wear gowns; parliamentary procedure is not always carefully observed; tempers are frequently lost; threats may even be made from time to time. These parties are adversaries; they are working out the most difficult issues which have always faced mankind: the control and division of wealth, as well as the imponderables of status and prestige. And what is more, the parties do not begin at some ideal point in their history, but rather after one group, which has already been entrenched in a position of power and status, is being challenged by an opposition that has been submerged and without power or status. At best, some conflict is inevitable, and one can only hope that some balance of power will be worked out as soon as possible, and that, gradually, a degree of accommodation and even cooperation will be achieved.

It is only natural under these circumstances that the going should be rough and uneven. It is for this reason that I have cautioned all along against the danger of overcommitment and of making social and moral pledges so vague that they may be impossible of fulfillment. The result may be frustration for everybody and even the growth of cynicism among executives who have tried and failed.

Uses of Power

Indeed, the carrying out of social and moral responsibility in complex situations is hardly ever a tidy, roseate affair except in utopian narratives. Ideas differ and the individuals concerned bring various degrees and kinds of power to implement their respective cases. This is true even in such a close-knit institution as the family, between husband and wife and between parents and children. And to the extent that the biological and emotional bond is weaker or entirely absent, power becomes increasingly a factor. It does not always have to be in the form of naked power, of actual coercive force. It may take the form of non-cooperation, or resistance, or pegging production, or the sheer moral power of invoking community sentiments of decency. Thus psychological warfare, employing propaganda and public relations techniques, has become a major strategy these days among nations, unions, corporations, and minority groups as they try to affect policies and courses of action in their favor.

For essentially no ready-made criteria are available to decide justice and equity in any given situation; these have to be worked out even as the parties are trying to resolve their differences. In time, of course, the parties develop a judicial procedure and eventually a constitutional framework, whether written or unwritten. This grows out of their meeting together and negotiating, bargaining, administering their settlements, handling grievances, and invoking arbitration. Even then the danger of resort to force is not eliminated. For we must remember that these are only supplementary constitutional systems, and as such, they are subject to at least as much strain as is the formal system of government established by the people through their representatives.

In our formal government, as we know, things get out of hand every once in a while in the halls of Congress and in administrative agencies, to the chagrin of all those who want to see the panoply of office maintained in full dignity. Even the Supreme Court has its off days. Rumor has it that the brethren are not without their human irritations at failure to convince each other as to the course of wisdom in the cases before them, an irritation that occasionally breaks out in the courtroom. Nor with all its prestige does the Court always succeed in having its judgment accepted immediately and without protest and resistance. Desegregation and Little Rock are reminders of the fragility of the constitutional process which seeks to replace the raw power of violence by the legitimate power of justice through law.

If this be true of our long-established, formal governmental system, is it any wonder that the newer, more informal framework of industrial constitutionalism is often disrupted by open conflicts?

Yet roughness and hard going should not lead to discouragement; they should only make one sober about goals and methods of attaining them. The wonder is that in spite of the primitive emotional elements in man and all the pulling and hauling, reason and morality should in the end prevail to propel men to work out amicable and peaceful ways of doing things together. Thus although no one should have any illusions about the difficulties, neither should he be discouraged from going forward. The chief test for those in management is to face squarely the fact that true morality means a sharing of power. Owners and managers have enjoyed unilateral power so long that they fail to realize that only by sharing it can they really be certain that justice will be done. In institutions as complex as the modern corporation, such sharing can best be effected within a constitutional framework.

Production Employees

Let us now take up the question asked in a previous chapter: what type of constitutionalism is appropriate for industry? It would obviously be foolhardy at this stage to try to draft a rigid and detailed blueprint without impairing the dynamic quality of industry, without destroying its capacity for creativeness. Constitutionalism here must be a matter of growth and experiment.

How about the form? Should policies be written or unwritten or partly written and partly unwritten?

When it comes to a large mass of people who have a tenuous claim on their jobs but who nevertheless depend on them for a living, as do wage earners paid by the hour or piece and subject to discharge or discipline, a written constitution is called for. Indeed, this is what has happened; the trade-union agreement is the way time and circumstance have answered the question. With the entry of unions as bargaining representatives of employees, the written trade-union agreement has become the base of the system of jurisprudence governing the work relationships of wage earners.

When the agreement expires, the workers have the right to strike. But when it is renewed, workers give up this right except under certain conditions which may be spelled out in the agreement. The constitutional system is set up to define wages, hours of work, leave of absence, holidays, vacations, seniority, promotions and demotions, safety regulations, a judicial machinery for handling grievances, and so forth.

We are dealing here with the largest single group in the typical corporation. The hourly employees are expandable and expendable, depending on economic conditions and profitability. They are looked upon as a primary cost in pricing goods and are therefore a strategic factor in the decision as to whether the company should make the particular goods, shut down, or move elsewhere. This group needs the full and complete protection of an agreement or contract. Constitutionalism calls here for a written document.

The White-collar Group

How about white-collar employees? Several groups are involved: clerical and office workers; scientists, engineers, and technicians; salesmen, foremen, and higher production supervisors; and those in top management. Unlike wage earners, these employees are on the monthly payroll, and closer to management. They have typically not sought union membership as a way of protecting their work relationship; they do not all need the same type of constitutional protection in the form of written policies or agreements. Nor have unions met a great degree of success in efforts to organize white-collar workers. Yet if justice is to be assured, all corporate employees should enjoy some guarantee of equality of treatment and have a way of redressing grievances.

Clerical workers constitute the largest single white-collar group. They are usually on a weekly basis, subject to layoff and replacement. They probably should have their conditions of employment spelled out in writing, including a grievance procedure with outside arbitration. They may even need some sort of organization, which may or may not be affiliated with a union. Most of the unions which have organized the production workers in heavy industry are also attempting to organize the office workers. In some companies they have succeeded and there is developing the same sort of constitutionalism as prevails for the hourly workers. In steel, for instance, it is becoming increasingly the custom for the office workers to be organized, but in separate locals belonging to the United Steelworkers of America.

Experience throughout the country, however, would indicate no great spontaneous reaching out toward trade unionism among clerical employees as a way of gaining status and fair conditions of employment. If managements give the necessary attention to the needs of these employees as a part of the corporate community—in actually writing out policies after full discussion—

the objective of constitutionalism may well be reached without trying to bring to bear the power of an outside, national organization.

Engineers and Technicians

We come next to a group of employees generally described as technical employees—scientists, engineers, and technicians. With advancing technology, these people are assuming an even greater importance in industry. The modern corporation must keep abreast of scientific discoveries and be alert to better ways of making old products as well as emerging new products. Scientists and engineers have been at a premium during the past two decades. Yet, in spite of the strategic position these men and women occupy, they are restless and discontented. In some companies they have formed unions. This may appear strange at first glance. Surely this group *should* be closely identified with management. Although they have received high starting salaries, a typical complaint one hears is that annual increases in salary are too small; another is that, in making promotions to higher positions, line men are preferred to the scientists and engineers who typically serve in a staff capacity; and still another complaint is that once hired, technical men are isolated in offices and laboratories and become the forgotten men of the company.

Surely technical personnel need close attention. For what is implicit in these complaints is a feeling that they are not part of the constitutional framework of the corporation. The conditions under which these employees serve and their opportunities should be spelled out, as policy for all to know. The larger the company, the more the need for this.

Suppose the technical staff desires to organize and deal collectively with management? The question is a perplexing one. Typically, top executives have looked upon members of this group as part of management. They are regarded as a source of future managerial talent. In a sense, scientists and engineers are hired as individuals and for their creative promise—not as members of an assembly line or a task where work is subdivided. Nevertheless, in some companies this group has grown so rapidly that a sentiment for organization and collective bargaining has arisen, much to the chagrin of management.

So far, most managers have looked askance at formal organization of, or collective bargaining with, scientists and engineers. But surely these people, with all their investment in higher education, and with all the skills they bring to the corporation, are entitled to know where they are, what they are entitled to, and where they are going. Their professional destiny should not be left entirely to the judgment of a few top men in the corporation.

Significantly, the secular trend in industry is for the white-collar group to outnumber the blue-collar workers. We may rest assured that this trend will continue. With mechanization, automation, computers, and new tools and processes, it becomes obvious that we shall need less brawn and fewer hands in industry and much more brains and skill. In other words, we are developing a new kind of middle class but without the traditional protections enjoyed by blue-collar employees over the years through unions and social legislation. If we are to avoid the tension, let alone the kind of strife which occurred when the blue-collar workers began to organize, we must be forehanded and work out a form of constitutionalism appropriate to the status and needs of this strategic and growing group so that it feels a greater identification with the corporation than has been true of the blue-collar workers.

The experience of another group is pertinent here. During the war, restlessness was so great among foremen that they organized a union with its center in the automotive industry. Strikes were declared. Under the rapid growth of industry during the war, top executives had overlooked the status and needs of their first-line management. No constitutional framework was provided for these key people. The result was a revolt.

The union which the foremen organized has now virtually gone out of business. Companies have increasingly addressed themselves to the problem. Policies have been spelled out in detail as to the conditions governing foremen. The results have been excellent. It is difficult to understand why foremen would want to organize a union. A strike is virtually doomed to failure, as was demonstrated in the Ford Motor Company in 1947. That the foremen revolted at all can be explained only on the grounds that, lacking a constitutional framework, they reached out for a power organization like a union.

The moral of all this is clear in dealing with scientific and technical personnel. Like the foremen and supervisors, these people may lack the drive that wage earners have to organize at any cost. But they do need a framework or system for dealing in an orderly, effective way with top management. Until such a framework is developed, there is no assurance that engineers and technicians will not resort to such strategies as did the foremen a few years ago. In fact, in a number of companies they are already organizing unions and are militant in pressing their case before management. Some have even walked out on strike.

Top Management

We come now to the higher officers: superintendents, division managers, vice-presidents, treasurers, comptrollers, and the rest. These men make up the top-management team. The group is small, and face-to-face relationships presumably prevail. A need for formal organization or for writing out policies hardly seems likely. Moreover, individual ability, creativeness, and resourcefulness are a prime consideration. Here we are looking for excellence in leadership and for the capacity to be on one's own in developing organization, products, policies. Nevertheless even here a constitutional posture should be maintained by the president of the company. Freedom of discussion, the right to due process—these should be an integral part of the corporation.

Indeed, in dealing with one another, with superiors and subordinates, and with staff members, all executives should act as if they were constitutional governors. This means that they should develop a negotiatory habit. They must not simply give orders, not just consult and listen, but actually learn *how* to negotiate—how to discern equities and rights, how to effect mutual exchanges to the end that settlements are worked out with a maximum of consensus by everyone involved.

What other elements of corporate constitutionalism should be considered in addition to the type of representation accorded various groups of staff workers and employees? Whether written or unwritten, the concept of a bill of rights must be included: freedom of speech, liberty of conscience, the right to petition, and the right to privacy. I do not mean to copy literally the Bill of Rights of our Federal Constitution; but I do believe that its spirit, with appropriate implementation, must become a living reality in the daily routine of a business.

An appropriate judicial system must surely be provided within the constitutional framework of a corporation. Production employees already enjoy such a system through the machinery provided in trade-union agreements. Similar machinery should be established for office employees, the technical and scientific group, and foremen. As for higher executives, they should be the kind of men who can talk things out with one another and work through their misunderstandings or grievances.

Arbitration

As part of the judicial system, there is no real substitute for arbitration by outsiders. Arbitration is becoming established more and more as the procedure to which parties resort when unable to agree, both in commercial and industrial cases. It is preferable to litigation before courts of law; the delays and expenses of legal procedures are avoided. Moreover, arbitration not only gives an opportunity to air a grievance, whether real or fancied, and arrive at a settlement, but it also helps to solidify the constitutional system. It develops over time a form of common law which becomes part of the customs and understandings of a mutual relationship. Perhaps no other function has made so large a contribution to the stabilization of management-union relationships as the provision for final arbitration in trade-union agreements.

Government, Opposition, Coalition

In one fundamental respect, corporate constitutionalism must differ from political constitutionalism. The executive cannot be removed by the employees. In other words, management as the government of the day is really a continuing government. Production workers and their unions constitute an opposition, but an opposition which can never take over office. To the extent that office workers, scientists, engineers, and others may set up machinery for handling differences and equities, they, too, will take on the function of an opposition, but only a continuing opposition. To subject the president, vice-presidents, and top-flight officers to plebiscites and votes of confidence would militate against the very efficiency of industry. To be successful, industry must be guided and directed by a management group enjoying flexibility and freedom. This is not to say that management should not be removed for inefficiency or misconduct, or for having lost the confidence of the work community. But such action had better be taken by stockholders and directors.

Indeed, although an opposition in the constitutional sense is desirable, it would be just as well to think of the actual structure in a typical corporation as a permanent coalition. The oppositions may raise questions, and even invoke procedures for protecting equities and redressing grievances. But since productivity, profitability, and survival, as well as justice, are prime considerations, the various groups must look upon themselves as an opposition within a framework of a coalition.

The Wider Coalition with Government

Just as management of a corporation is to be considered as the government of the day functioning in the atmosphere of a constitutional coalition not only with the trade unions but with other groups, so each corporation must accept the fact that it must live in a position of opposition and coalition with government. Government may be critical of corporations and set up rules for business conduct, and corporations may understandably be critical of government. Nevertheless, instead of regarding government as an enemy, business leaders should look upon themselves as living in a state of perpetual coalition with it. In our modern, large-scale interdependent society, government and only government can handle the serious problems of maladjustment that inevitably arise in our decentralized private economy, such as unemployment, old age, and sickness. Similarly, government is the only agency that can formulate and enforce acceptable practices of fair competition among corporations. What is called for here really is a strategy of combined operation among corporations, unions, and government.

Now that the rough-and-tumble stage of union organization and the bitter fights, strikes, sit-downs, and mass picketing are over, and now that an accommodation has been reached, it has become fashionable for management to say, "We may as well realize that unions are here to stay." It would be just as well for management to recognize that government is here to stay, too. And what is more, perhaps also to recognize that the welfare state is here to stay. The acceptance of public responsibility for the hazards of modern life has by this time become a world-wide phenomenon. It is not likely that the trend will ever be reversed. It therefore behooves businessmen to become friendly critics but not opponents of government intervention.

28

Conclusion

THE year 1776 marked the emergence of three great events destined to determine the fate of the nation.

First was the Declaration of Independence, which dedicated government to the freedom and welfare of man.

Second was Watt's steam engine. It marked the beginning of modern technology and the substitution of machine power for human drudgery. It presaged ultimately automation, electronics, computers, increasing mastery of nature's power, and the realization of abundance instead of the scarcity which had always confronted society.

Third was the publication of Adam Smith's *Wealth of Nations,* which raised self-interest and private initiative, as against government-dictated activity, to the highest pinnacle of legitimacy. It became the dominant economic philosophy of our nation during the nineteenth and early twentieth centuries.

It is the forces, ideas, and allegiances around these three seminal events that have made up the strands in the weaving of our national society. For the first 150 years, technology and economics dominated the scene, under the leadership of business. A new country, with great resources, spanning a continent, together with a new people, coming in large numbers to escape tyranny and restrictions, constituted an ideal setting for self-interest and private initiative. The country developed rapidly and wealth accumulated. But success was shadowed by poverty and maladjustment; mansions and skyscrapers were surrounded by slums.

During this first century and a half, the Declaration of Independence served primarily the pride of the nation—a symbol to be invoked on holidays or times of crisis. It was inevitable that with the maturing and affluence of the nation as the twentieth century advanced, and under the shock of a great depression, the ideology of the Declaration of Independence should pass beyond the stage of symbolism to that of practical policy. So, all of a sudden, the welfare state sprung almost full grown into life with the enactment of massive social legislation to provide for the human problems of a productive, dynamic capitalism.

Business has gradually accepted—slowly, to be sure, but step by step—the measures enacting social insurance, minimum wages, collective bargaining with unions, responsibility for human relationships, and the whole idea of an inextricable interrelationship between the prosperity of business and the welfare of the whole community.

What is needed now is a maturing of the experience of the past quarter-century into a complete realization that business, labor, and government are engaged in a permanent coalition, a combined operation to fulfill the destiny of the moral as well as the material greatness promised at the beginning of the nation.

Against one hazard, the responsible business executive must be on constant guard—the danger of disillusionment and even cynicism.

The long history of mankind cautions against the expectation of any easy fulfillment of moral aspirations in the here and now. Thus revolution and war, even when crowned with victory, frequently result in the defeat of the spirit. The struggle in itself may evoke vision and sacrifice. The aftermath may well be counterrevolution, terror, and corruption. Camus traces eloquently this degradation of man in *The Rebel;* Orwell and Huxley make it vivid in fictional sociology through *1984* and *Brave New World.*

Though the West withstood and freed the world from the onslaught of Nazi tyranny, the men who won the victory on the battlefield became the "beat generation" in this country, and the "angry young men" in Britain. Our literature is streaked with self-flagellation. Our very success in creating wealth for mankind and in bringing the abolition of poverty within reach is turned into an indictment of materialism and sensualism.

Under such circumstances it is tempting to give up and retreat to self-interest. But for those who would lead, retreat is impossible. Unless the new and rapidly growing management group holds on to social and moral goals, it is doomed to lose what it now has in the way of authority and opportunity. Private enterprise in the form of the modern corporation has still to win the prize of legitimacy. The prize will continue to prove elusive without a growing faith in the community that, whatever the faltering, justice and the good life can best be realized through a decentralized industrial system manned by individuals of high purpose responsive to the ethics of our Judaeo-Christian tradition.

The fulfillment of the promise of this tradition is a long and seemingly tortuous road. Saints and martyrs have suffered and even perished on it. The very people they sought to free and succor, stoned and tortured them. It is not given us to understand the saint and sinner in every man; this duality which makes man noble, or evil, or capable of both good and evil under varying time and circumstances.

We in our own recent times have created the state, the corporation, the union—all to fulfill and ennoble man. It has not always worked out that way.

Have we been guilty of overromanticizing the saintly side

of man, forgetting the demonic in everyone? Have we set up a standard of perfectibility impossible of realization on this mortal earth?

Surely businessmen, accustomed as they are to all the grim realities they face every day in building and operating economic institutions, should be the last to suffer discouragement. Perhaps what they can best bring to the quest for justice and equity is the same hardheadedness that they would apply to their daily jobs in getting things done amidst uncertainty and risk. But they too must be shielded from the natural temptations to become arbitrary, capricious, and punitive—a temptation consequent upon disillusionment with their people. That is why we need some organized framework to assure a way of justice which accepts yet transcends man's fallibility and sinfulness. Hence the urgency of a framework of constitutionalism for the modern corporation.

And yet constitutionalism by itself is not enough. Justice and equity must be carried beyond the requirements of the letter. Problems arise when feelings are injured; people suffer injustices of a nature that cannot be covered by a written document or policy. Unless equity is done, constitutionalism loses its vitality. Although a business cannot be expected to function as a church or a family or a clinic, human values cannot be ignored without peril.

Indeed, the great corporation executive, as any great governor of men, is he who so conveys justice and equity in all his bearing that his people know that righteousness prevails within his realm.